The Boys Who Were Left Behind

THE
BOYS
WHO
WERE
LEFT

The 1944 World Series
between the Hapless
St. Louis Browns and
the Legendary
St. Louis Cardinals

John Heidenry
& Brett Topel

University of Nebraska Press   Lincoln & London

© 2006 by John Heidenry
and Brett Topel
All rights reserved
Manufactured in the
United States of America

⊗

Library of Congress Cataloging-
in-Publication Data
Heidenry, John.
The boys who were left behind:
the 1944 World Series between
the hapless St. Louis Browns and
the legendary St. Louis Cardinals /
John Heidenry and Brett Topel.
p.   cm.
Includes bibliographical references and index.
ISBN-13: 978-0-8032-2428-5 (cloth: alk. paper)
ISBN-10: 0-8032-2428-1 (cloth: alk. paper)
1. World Series (Baseball) (1944)
2. St. Louis Browns (Baseball team)—History.
3. St. Louis Cardinals (Baseball team)—History.
4. Baseball—Missouri—St. Louis—History—
20th century.
I. Topel, Brett.   II. Title.
GV878.4.H45   2006
796.357'64'0977866—dc22
2005019237

In memory of my brother
Richard Anson Heidenry
JH

To Emily,
The captain of my team
BT

CONTENTS

ILLUSTRATIONS

The Boys Who Were Left Behind

Win One for the Georgia Peach

The most exciting, improbable, and strangest World Series that baseball had ever seen was only four innings away when Chet Laabs, a chunky St. Louis Browns outfielder, strode to the plate in the bottom of the fifth inning. The day was Sunday, October 1, 1944, and the place was Sportsman's Park in a fading neighborhood on the North Side of St. Louis, Missouri.

The Browns, a collection of misfits, 4-FS, brawlers, and drunks, and indisputably the worst team in the history of baseball, stood at that very moment on the verge of the sport's greatest upset. In three straight late September games, they had somehow, almost miraculously, defeated the New York Yankees, winners of the American League pennant the past three years and without question the greatest team ever in baseball. Now, in the final game of the regular season, the score was tied 2 to 2. If the Browns could complete a four-game sweep against the Yankees, they would not only capture their first flag, after more than forty years of loitering in the cellar, but also become the sport's all-time Cinderella team.

The story of the Yankees in 1944 was no less extraordinary than that of the Browns. They had lost virtually every member of their Hall of Fame–studded 1941 and 1943 championship teams, yet were able to stay in the race for most of the season. By September 15 they had even taken over first place. One important reason for their run for the crown was manager Joe McCarthy, who had a reputation for staying cool in tough situations.

Although this was not the Yankees team that fans were accustomed to, the roster still included such outstanding players as infielders George Henry "Snuffy" Stirnweiss and Nick Etten and outfielder Johnny Lindell. Stirnweiss was to finish the season with a batting average of .319, and his teammate Herschel Martin batted .302. The New Yorkers had failed that year, for the first time in twenty years, to hit 100 homers, managing only 96, but they still posed a formidable threat. Yet, indisputably, the absence of such stellar sluggers as Joe DiMaggio, who was missing his second season, catcher Bill Dickey, and outfielder Charlie Keller had taken its toll. No team had capitalized on the Yankees' wartime weakness more than the Browns. With Laabs now at the plate, they were closing in for the kill—and the American League pennant.

The Boston Red Sox had been the first Browns rival to fall by the wayside. At the beginning of September, the team was in fourth place, though only 3 ½ games behind St. Louis. But their unfortunate history was riddled with one bad break after another, and the 1944 pennant race was to be no exception. When, late in the campaign, the Selective Service tapped second baseman Bobby Doerr (.325), third baseman Jim Tabor (.285), and star pitcher Tex Hughson (17-5, 2.26), the Boston team quickly faded.

Like the Red Sox, the Detroit Tigers were usually mired in the second division, especially since Hank Greenberg had left in 1941. Then, in mid-July, slugger Dick Wakefield temporarily returned from the service and led his team into contention, whacking 12 homers, batting in 53, and hitting .355 in only 78 games. Wakefield had been away from baseball since the end of the 1943 season, when he entered the Navy's aviation cadet program, only to return when the curriculum was discontinued. At the same time, the Tigers' lackluster offense was offset by the pitching staff's dynamic duo, Hal Newhouser (29-9, 2.72) and Dizzy Trout (17-14, 2.12).

Both the Tigers and the Browns had identical 87-65 records going into the final weekend of the season. The St. Louis team faced the tougher road, having to play the defending champions, the New York Yankees, while the Tigers faced off against the also-ran Senators. Both the Browns and the Tigers won on the second-to-last day of the season, setting up a last-day-of-the-season showdown, with both teams still tied for first place.

If St. Louis's collection of baseball leftovers were unable to complete their magical season successfully, and the Yankees came through in the clutch with a season-ending victory, as just about everyone expected except the Browns themselves, they would go down as a footnote in baseball history—a team that almost pulled off the impossible but characteristically lost heart in the last few innings. After all, they were the only team in baseball history that had never won a pennant—or even come close.

Yet there was one baseball eminence who did believe in the Browns all throughout that long, wacky, first-and-last-of-its-kind season. As the red-hot pennant race was heading into the home stretch in September, Browns manager Luke Sewell assembled his club in the visitors' locker room in Cleveland. Sewell wanted to read a letter from his good friend Ty Cobb. One of the greatest players in baseball history, the Georgia Peach told Sewell and his men that he was rooting for them to win the pennant and knew that they could do it. It was a tall order. The previous year, the Browns had finished in sixth place, twenty-five games behind the indomitable Yankees, This year, though, under Sewell's masterful direction in his fourth season as manager, the Browns had been in first place seven times since opening day, for a dizzying total of 128 days; nor were they ever worse than in third place, which they held for two days in May, and again in early September.

Now, on the final day of the regular season, the Browns found themselves tied for first place with Cobb's former team. At that very moment, the Tigers were playing the Washington Senators in Washington—a game that had started one hour earlier than the Browns game because of the difference in time zones.

Before the start of his game, Sewell had been sitting as usual in the right corner of the Browns' dugout, watching the Yankees working out and occasionally glancing up at the scoreboard. He seemed nervous. The outcome of the Tigers-Senators game was almost as important as that of the Browns-Yankees game. If the Tigers were victorious, and the Browns defeated the Yankees, the Browns and Tigers would then play a one-game, winner-take-all playoff game in Detroit the very next day. Already, the Browns players had packed their bags, and arrangements had been made to transport the team to the train station for the trip up to Detroit immediately after the game—not a very hopeful sign.

What fans in both Detroit and St. Louis were witnessing on that fall afternoon was what one sportswriter called "the rarest thing known to baseball—a major-league pennant race carried down to the final day of the season." Only three times before had that happened in the century: in 1908, when the Tigers met the Chicago White Sox on the last day and won; in 1934, when the Cardinals clinched the flag on the closing day of the season; then in 1942, when the Cardinals once again won by taking the first game of a final Sunday doubleheader. This final day included two games, four teams, and two time zones.

A thirty-two-year-old left fielder who stood five foot eight, Laabs had arms like Popeye's. His hero-worshipping son, six-year-old Chester, was sitting in the stadium, wearing a hand-me-down batboy's white home uniform with the club's distinctive brown-orange piping. Every other team in baseball wore combinations of white and gray, blue, black, or red. Only the Browns wore, well, brown. But this team was like that. They always did things their way, which in their fifty-two years in the American League usually meant not for the best. As sportswriter Joe Falls once remarked, "They looked more like a softball team than a baseball team, but that was okay. They were different. They were allowed to look different. They were always in last place."

Usually battling them for last place were the Philadelphia Athletics and the Washington Senators. But for sheer ability to lock up the bottom rung in the ladder, nobody excelled better than the Browns. Year after year, they made losing almost a ritual. Yet it was hard to dislike this carefree, happy bunch. At least off the field, nobody had a better time.

Laabs, almost more than any other member of the 1944 roster, was doing his best to help the Browns keep up their losing ways. Though hardworking and earnest, he had one fatal flaw. He struck out too much. Before 1944, the biggest moment of his career had been the time, back when he was with the Detroit Tigers, when he struck out five times in a game and helped Bob Feller of the Cleveland Indians set a major-league record with eighteen strikeouts. Whenever fans talked about Laabs, that was what most of them remembered. A quiet, pleasant man, Laabs always got embarrassed when anyone mentioned that game against Feller, yet he never got angry. He accepted that moment as his probable only mention in baseball history, and sometimes even poked fun at himself. But now, as he stood at the plate in the most important game of his life, the free-swinging, right-handed Laabs was about to rewrite the record book one more time and put an end forever to his being the butt of strikeout jokes.

There had even been a bit of booing when Laabs was announced as the starting left fielder for the Browns. Perhaps what some fans forgot was that in 1942 Laabs had driven in 99 runs and hit 27 home runs, finishing second in homers only to Ted Williams, who hit 36. On the other hand, up until this game with the Yankees, Laabs had hit only 3 home runs for the year—the fourth one, in fact, as recently as the previous inning in this very game against the Yankees. The odds of Laabs repeating that performance and bringing the Browns a pennant, as he now stood at the plate in the bottom half of the fifth inning, were, to say the least, astronomical. The St. Louis Browns had never once surprised their fans with a miracle.

When Laabs had first arrived in St. Louis, back on June 1, the team's vice president, Bill DeWitt, had arranged a job for his newest ballplayer at his father-in-law's local plant, which made pipes for the war. Laabs's job was to inspect the pipes; he later learned they were being sent down to the uranium-enrichment plant in Oak Ridge, Tennessee, to be used as part of the atom bomb project.

But having a full-time day job meant that Laabs was limited to playing part-time ball with the team, night and Sunday games only. Often his job kept him so busy that he was not even able to take batting practice, and he would arrive at the ballpark literally minutes before game time. Realizing that he was never going to do justice to the Browns, or to himself, under that schedule, Laabs finally quit his war-plant job in August to devote himself entirely to playing baseball—his profession since 1935, when he had begun playing with a Fort Wayne, Indiana, team in the Three-I League. While quitting his job did help a little, he had not developed again into the feared batter he had been in years past.

Like Laabs, the rest of the Browns team had similar semivagrant histories. Of the eight men on the first string, five others besides Laabs had been shucked off by other teams. Right fielder Gene Moore was an ex-Brooklyn Dodger and Boston Brave; left fielder Mike Kreevich was a washed-up Chicago White Sox; George McQuinn, at first base, had puddled around the Yankees' farm system while waiting for Lou Gehrig to slow down; Don Gutteridge, at second, once played with the Cardinals; third baseman Mark Christman was a former shortstop for the Detroit Tigers.

The eyes of 37,815 fans, the biggest crowd in the stadium's history, were all fastened on Laabs on this October day. Another 15,000 fans had been turned away. But none watched with more breathless excitement than little Chester, who was praying for a miracle. He wanted his dad to hit another home run, just like the one he had smashed 400 feet off the scoreboard in left center field in the fourth inning. Up until now, that homer had been the most dramatic moment in the almost unbearably tense four-game series with the Yankees.

The day for this climactic battle was a typical midwestern fall afternoon: a broiling sun, the thermometer in the high eighties, and a shirt-sleeved crowd. Many of the men in the stands were wearing straw boaters. The Browns management had futilely attempted to round up the 105 ushers scheduled to work the game in order to open the park at nine that morning, instead of at one o'clock; in the end, the gates opened at noon, and within an hour all seats were taken. Many of those who managed to get inside the park were unable to force their way to the grandstands. Ushers were reduced to bystanders as crowds jammed into every entrance aisle. Some of those who squeezed into the stadium had to satisfy themselves with listening to the game being broadcast on radios on the counters of concession booths, while hundreds of others were packed into an aisle where they could follow the progress of the game only by seeing hits, errors, runs, and outs being posted on the left field scoreboard.

Among the fans sitting in the seats was one of baseball's immortals, Rogers Hornsby, who had once managed both the Browns and the St. Louis Cardinals. In 1926 he had brought the latter their first National League pennant and World Series title. Almost certainly, like every other St. Louisan, he was rooting for the Browns—if only so that St. Louis could host the first ever World Series to be played entirely on the banks of the Mississippi River. If the Browns won the American League pennant, they would be playing none other than the Cardinals, their fearsome hometown rivals, for the championship of the world. Stranger things had happened—though given the history of the hapless, abysmally incompetent Browns, perhaps not.

Baseball, it is probably safe to say, was America's greatest diversion during this dark period when a world war was being waged in both Europe and the Pacific. But it was not the only diversion. As the 1944 season got under way, comic strip hero Dick Tracy was pursuing a villain named Flattop aboard a ship, with Flattop sneaking away in a rowboat, leaving behind his partner, Vitamin. Little Orphan Annie, meanwhile, was staying with a virtuous woman named Mazie who had rented her parlor to a man named Sinsin the Swami, who read minds and confided to Annie that he knew her old ally, Punjab. Pensive, a 7 to 1 shot, had won the Kentucky Derby. By coincidence, the big Hollywood movie that year was *Meet Me in St. Louis*, a musical about the 1904 World's Fair starring twenty-two-year-old Judy Garland.

Nothing, though, in those pretelevision days quite offered Americans, both on the home front and in the theaters of war, the respite from anxiety, hardship, and grief that the national pastime did. Just 117 days earlier, on the sixth day of June, D-day, Allied forces had stormed the beaches of Normandy to begin the invasion of Europe. Already the U.S. First Army was advancing into Germany toward Aachen, Goebbels and Himmler were trying in vain to rally the German people to rise up and resist the invaders farmhouse by farmhouse, and Marshall Pétain of Vichy France was being charged with treason. British prime minister Winston Churchill had hinted that Hitler would not be put on trial but condemned to death by executive decree. Yet millions of U.S. servicemen around the world, who had introduced baseball to thousands of bases, towns, and cities in Europe and Asia, took the time to listen via short-wave radio to a faraway contest that pitted the sport's Goliath and David—the damn Yankees and the impotent Browns—in the westernmost outpost of both the American and National leagues.

During September, Sewell had basically used a four-man starting pitching rotation. The three regulars were Jack Kramer, Nelson Potter, and Denny Galehouse, while Bob Muncrief and Sigmund "Jack" Jakucki shared the fourth spot. For the season finale against the Yankees, Sewell's choices were limited. Both Potter and Kramer had pitched in the doubleheader two days earlier, while Galehouse had thrown just the day before. Muncrief's arm was bothering him. Two other pitchers, Al Hollingsworth and Tex Shirley, had been inconsistent, and Sewell had not used either one since July 21 and August 18, respectively.

In Detroit, manager Steve O'Neill was taking no chances, electing to use against the Senators one of his starters on just one day's rest. Sewell, though, could not make up his mind whether to save one of his premier starters for the one-game playoff in Detroit, which he assumed was a strong likelihood. Chatting with Zack Taylor, the pitching coach, the day before the game, he asked, "Are we going to pitch one of these guys out of turn or pitch Jakucki?" Then one of them was overheard to say, "Goddamn it, pitch Jakucki. He's due up. Pitch him. And if they start hitting him, we can always take him out. But start him." Even though Jakucki's arm was tired, Sewell chose to go with the thirty-five-year-old Jakucki, the wildest card in the Browns' deck of jokers.

Jakucki had done reasonably well for the Browns that season, winning 12 games and losing 9 in his previous 34 games, 23 of them starts (of which he completed 11). It was not the quality of his pitching, though, that concerned his teammates. It was his drinking. On a team known for its hard partyers, Jakucki was the unrivaled star. Muncrief, Shirley, and Sam Zoldak also had reputations as drinkers, but only Jakucki could invariably be found in a bar if he was not in a game.

Sig Jakucki gave his word to coaches that he would not drink the night before
the regular season finale against the Yankees. He never said anything, however,
about the morning of the game. (Arteaga Photos)

"I wouldn't say [Jakucki was] an alcoholic, but he drank a lot," Galehouse later charitably recalled. "He was a barfly."

Not only was he a drinker, but Jakucki was also a brawler. "He was a
mean son of a bitch, a big, strong bastard that would turn over a juke
joint every night if he could, you know," another teammate, Ellis Clary,
remembered. "And he got into all kinds of crap. He got beat up, but in
the process he wounded a few people along the way. He's a tough son of
a bitch, but he was a mean monkey. But you couldn't help but like him
if he was on your side. He was a fun guy, but gee, at night he'd get a few
belts and turn over a joint somewhere. No matter where he was, he'd get
in trouble."

Only recently, in fact, while the Browns were battling the Yankees in
New York, Jakucki had been drinking one night at the Travelers Bar across
the street from the New Yorker Hotel, where the Browns were staying.
Another customer came in, sat on the stool next to Jakucki, and started
an argument. Words got so heated that the man eventually pulled a gun,
stuck it into Jakucki's ribs, and threatened to blow him off the stool. But

Jakucki merely grabbed the gun, pulled his own gun, knocked the guy flat on his back with it, threw the man's gun down beside him, and walked out. Subsequently word got around that the man Jakucki had kayoed was a mobster.

The main thing Sewell and the other Browns now had to worry about was that Jakucki not ply himself with drinks with that right hand before the all-important fourth game with the Yankees. When the team was in St. Louis, many of the players stayed at the Melbourne Hotel, a modest midtown hotel on Grand Avenue and Lindell Boulevard, just a ten-minute drive from the stadium. The night after they had miraculously won their third straight game against the Yankees, some of the players got together in the lobby to discuss whether they might not be better off with another pitcher on the mound the next day. One of Jakucki's few defenders was coach Taylor, who said that whether or not Jakucki drank that night, he would still give the Yankees all they could handle.

Some of the players, along with Taylor, were still hanging out in the lobby when Jakucki rolled in with a bottle of whiskey wrapped up in a brown bag.

"You're not going to take that to your room!" Taylor yelled at him.

"I tell you, I won't drink tonight," Jakucki solemnly replied. "I promise you I won't take a drink tonight. But don't try to take the liquor away, or there'll be trouble."

The next morning when Bob Bauman, the Browns trainer, was working on Jakucki, he noticed alcohol on his breath and reminded him of his promise.

"I kept my promise last night," Jakucki advised him. "I told you I wouldn't take a drink last night, but I didn't promise I wouldn't take one this morning."

The pregame tension in the Browns dugout visibly dissipated when umpire Ed Rommel walked through, imitating a blind man, with eyes closed and arms extended. Some players laughed, and another yelled out, tongue in cheek, "You never could see beyond the end of your nose." Rommel had once pitched for the Philadelphia Athletics and had appeared in two World Series games back in the twenties.

Infielder Ellis Clary also helped ease the tension. A rabid Chicago Bears fan, he hid a radio in the dugout before the game. Whenever Sewell went out to the third-base line to coach, according to teammate Gutteridge, Clary would sneak out his radio, plug it in, and listen to the football game. Clary's covert passion helped everyone else relax. When they were not watching the game against the Yankees, they peppered Clary with questions: "Hey, what they'd do?" And Clary would give a play-by-play description of the latest football action. As soon as Sewell headed back to the dugout, Clary switched off the radio and hid it behind him again.

Al Zarilla was another player who helped his Browns teammates steady their nerves. The outfielder eventually hoped to turn professional golfer. Since the clubhouse contained a box of sand that everyone used to spit tobacco into, Zarilla had brought along a golf club and would stand in the sand, practicing his swing.

Spirits in the Browns dugout remained high after the game began. All the players were yelling themselves hoarse, urging on their teammates, whether at bat or on the field. The Yankees, in contrast, like the champions they were, maintained their accustomed professional composure, talking in normal conversational tones or occasionally whistling through their fingers or applauding when the game was going their way.

As with the previous three games in the series, Sewell had filled out his lineup card in the same way, batting his catcher eighth. He selected Red Hayworth over Frank Mancuso, and installed George McQuinn at first base, though McQuinn was not batting well of late and was now hitting sixth instead of third.

For middle infielders, Sewell relied as usual on Don Gutteridge at second base and also designated him the leadoff batter, and he kept shortstop Vern Stephens as the cleanup batter. Mark Christman, who played third, batted seventh.

Sewell also put Gene Moore in right field and batted him fifth, instead of Milt Byrnes, who had played and batted in that position and order in the doubleheader of September 29. In center field was Kreevich, who batted second, as he had done in seventeen of the last nineteen outings. The one player Sewell had not been sure of was Laabs. Though Laabs had been playing more ball than usual in September, Sewell had decided to bench him for the New York series, until he saw him swinging the bat during batting practice before the doubleheader, and changed his mind. Sewell thought Laabs hadn't swung the bat so well all season, and on a hunch put him in left field and batted him third.

The Browns were facing a formidable Yankee lineup: Stirnweiss at second base, Bud Metheny in right field, and Martin in left. Lindell anchored the outfield in center, and slugger Nick Etten played first base. Frank Crosetti, Oscar Grimes, and Mike Garbark rounded out the New York position players, while Mel Queen got the nod on the mound.

Six of the nine starters had played on the Yankees' 1943 World Series championship team. Of the remaining three, Mike Garbark was a rookie, and Martin, out of the majors since 1940, had been hitting .298 with 11 doubles, 3 triples, and 9 homers in just 84 games. Queen, though only 6-2 for the year, had allowed just 64 hits in 77 innings.

Up in Detroit, before the start of the other big game of the day, high drama had preceded the first pitch between the Tigers and Senators. Dutch Leonard, a thirty-five-year-old knuckleballer with a 13-14 record that year, was pitching for the Senators opposite the Tigers' Dizzy Trout. That morning, before game time, an unidentified man had called Leonard at the Book-Cadillac Hotel, where the team was staying.

"Hello, Dutch," the man said. "You're pitching today, aren't you?"

"Yeah, I guess so," Leonard replied, assuming the caller was someone from his hometown in southern Illinois; with the war on, many people had come to Detroit to work in the factories.

"Good," said the man. "You have a chance to make a lot of money."

"What do you mean?"

"I'm authorized to offer you better than $20,000 if you don't have a good day."

Not quite understanding what was going on, Leonard again asked, "What do you mean?"

The man repeated his offer, and only then did it dawn on Leonard that the caller probably represented a gambling syndicate.

"Go to hell," he said, and hung up.

Shaken, Leonard later confided what had happened to his teammate George Case, telling him he thought it was just a prank. But Case convinced Leonard to tell someone in management. When the team reached Briggs Stadium, Leonard told coach Clyde Milan what had happened, and Milan immediately informed manager Ossie Bluege. Uncertain whether he would be allowed to pitch, Leonard waited until Milan returned from his conversation with Bluege, handed him a brand-new baseball, and told him to begin warming up.

Back in St. Louis, things seemed to be going the Yankees' way from the beginning. With two out in the first inning, Martin tripled off the right field fence. Then Lindell, the cleanup hitter, hit a bounding ball to the right of the shortstop. Though Stephens fielded it well enough, he tossed it high over McQuinn's head to give the Yankees the lead.

Then in the third inning, after Queen fanned, Christman nervously tried to catch Stirnweiss's easy roller and instead kicked it all the way

Chet Laabs is greeted at home plate after belting one of his two home runs against the Yankees on the final day of the season. (Arteaga Photos)

from third base to the pitcher's mound, enabling Stirnweiss to reach first safely. He then stole his fifty-fifth base of the season, and added insult to injury by skipping to third when catcher Hayworth fired the ball into center field for the third Browns error in three innings. Then Martin got another hit, blasting a double to right field, just missing a home run, and easily scoring Stirnweiss for a 2 to 0 Yankee lead.

Browns fans were eager for a rally at the top of the fourth. Queen, a right-hander, had kept the Browns hitless in the first three innings with his sizzling fastball. Stepping up first at the plate was Kreevich, who promptly belted a line-drive single into left field. Then Laabs lashed a pitch eight rows deep into the left field bleachers to tie the game 2 to 2. "The echo of the roar from the crowd must have carried right on to Detroit," one reporter remarked.

Only then, as Laabs circled the bases, did the scoreboard keeper decide it was time to post the final score from Detroit, Senators 4, Tigers 1. The crowd erupted, and the hooting went on for more than five minutes. Finally, for the first time in the long, dismal history of the Browns franchise, a pennant and an all–St. Louis World Series was in sight—only five innings away.

In the home fifth inning, Queen retired the first two batters, seemingly having cooled down the Browns' hot hitting of the previous inning. But then Kreevich again ripped a single. That brought up Laabs, now facing Queen for the third time in the contest. On this occasion, a chastened Queen decided to throw a curveball, a pitch Laabs always had difficulty hitting. But not this time, and he launched the ball 400 feet into the left center field seats. The blast gave the Browns a 4 to 2 lead and the long-elusive pennant finally seemed not just within reach, but *theirs*.

In the eighth inning, Stephens bought the Browns some insurance when he hit his twentieth home run of the season over the right field pavilion. Going into the ninth, Jakucki had a 5 to 2 lead. "Sensing the dramatics of the situation, he strolled slowly out to the mound, soaking in the atmosphere and electricity that was buzzing throughout the crowd."

The first half of the ninth was as nail-biting as anything that had gone before. Lindell blasted a pitch. The crowd held its collective breath as what seemed like a certain homer headed for the center field bleachers. Moore had to run all the way to the wall, but just shy of the fence the ball plopped into his glove. The crowd sighed with relief. Etten then hit a single past Gutteridge at second base, but Jakucki got Crosetti to line out to Kreevich in center field for the second out.

Then Grimes stepped into the batter's box. Sewell was to remember what happened next as the most memorable play of his career.

"Grimes sent a high twisting foul toward the Yankee bullpen," he recalled, "about 50 or 75 feet high, and about 10 feet outside of first base."

"Squeeze it, George! Squeeze it, George!" Gutteridge was shouting, running over from first base.

There was hardly a sound until McQuinn found the ball firmly in his glove. Immediately, he and Gutteridge were swamped by their teammates and by the thousands of delirious fans who jumped over the wall and ran onto the field, where they began snake-dancing around the bases in celebration. An exultant Galehouse, as people swarmed around him, thought with satisfaction, "This is why I quit my job!" Torn programs and newspapers filled the air, fluttering down from the upper grandstand seats. It took some of the Browns players fifteen minutes to fight their way to the dugout on the third-base line. Some eager fans even tried to burst into the Browns dugout to congratulate the players, but police stopped them.

The Browns, who had started the season 9-0 but then fell out of first place, regained it, then slipped out again, had had to fight a whispering campaign all season long that sooner or later they would fall by the wayside. Now they had proved once and for all that they were champions. The courageous castoffs had won eleven of their last dozen games and now were heading for the World Series and destiny.

"To the Browns went the American League pennant in one of the most stirring climax drives in all the annals of the game," wrote New York–based sportswriter Dan Daniel.

Agreeing with him was John Drebinger of the *New York Times*, who wrote, "It was perhaps the most dramatic finish any championship campaign has ever known, one which even the most gifted scenario expert could scarcely have improved on."

At the end of the day, a ragtag ball team pieced together from remnants discarded by nearly every other team in baseball had won the greatest and closest pennant race in the history of the American League. The game ended at exactly 3:38 p.m. by the clock atop the left field scoreboard.

The celebration continued in the clubhouse. Laabs and Jakucki, who had allowed just six hits and one walk while striking out four, hugged each other. Tears of joy were streaming down the cheeks of Browns owner Don Barnes, who kissed the baseball responsible for the final out. Champagne and beer were flowing. While the players celebrated, their luggage was still sitting in another part of the clubhouse, ready for that trip to Detroit that was never to happen. Jakucki made it official when he tore up the sign listing the travel plans for the train ride.

Enthusiasm was running so high that even batboy Bobby Scanlon, who also was a batboy for the Cardinals, walked up to Barnes and kissed him on the cheek. Barnes in turn swung around and smacked Laabs behind the ear. Other players were hugging and smacking Kreevich.

At one point, Jakucki went over to McQuinn, who had held onto the ball that ended the game as though it were a gold nugget. Wiping the sweat off his brow, Jakucki grimly wrapped an arm around his teammate's shoulder and said, "Look, pal, that ball means a lot to me. How about giving it to me?"

McQuinn's face dropped.

"Well," he said, "let's be neighborly about this thing. I'll give you half of it."

Barnes, overhearing the argument, told Scanlon, "Fetch me a saw, son."

Moments later, Jakucki and McQuinn spent ten minutes trying to hack the ball in two with a saw. But the ball remained infuriatingly intact, if somewhat battered. Finally, Scanlon pulled out the quarter that Laabs had tipped him for running off to get a soda, and flipped it. The coin fell heads up, and McQuinn got to keep his thoroughly chewed up ball.

All this time, while his teammates laughed, danced, and kissed each other, Laabs sat silently in front of his locker, wiping a towel across his face and looking at the floor as if in a daze, perhaps wondering whether it could possibly be true that he, the big bust during the season, the perennial benchwarmer, the weekend substitute, was now not only the man of the hour but a man who had just made baseball history.

Yankee manager Joe McCarthy stopped by the locker room and told Sewell, "You fellows played great ball against us, and if you stick to that pace you'll take those Cardinals just as well."

Outside the park, thousands of joyful fans were breaking into spontaneous demonstrations. Immediately after the game one group tied washtubs and tin cans onto the back of their cars and drove through the nearby midtown theater district. But gasoline rationing soon put an end to their jubilation. A group of young people later tried to get another parade under way downtown, but their spirits were dampened when two policemen began taking down license numbers and sternly warned them about losing their gas-rationing coupons for indulging in such frivolity.

Many of the fans "were unashamedly weeping," the St. Louis Post-Dispatch reported. At parties around town after the game, Browns fans no doubt also toasted the Senators. The Browns and Senators had gotten into a few brawls during the season, but the Senators refused to hold a grudge and had beaten the Tigers twice.

The city itself, though, took the historic occasion calmly. After all, there was a war on. The same day that the Browns won their last game against the Yankees, the Associated Press reported that Soviet planes had swarmed over Yugoslavia in around-the-clock raids on German forces, who were fiercely defending their Balkan lifeline southeast of the capital, Belgrade. Also, it was a Sunday, and most places were closed, especially taverns. The Browns did hold a team party at the Chase Hotel, the city's

Manager Luke Sewell, whose transformation of the Browns from perennial losers to champions was nothing short of miraculous. (National Baseball Hall of Fame Library, Cooperstown NY)

swankiest. But the curfew was early because there was still a World Series to play.

When Sewell won the pennant, he created a small domestic problem for himself. Such was the gentlemanly nature of baseball back in 1944 that both he and Billy Southworth, the Cardinals' manager, and their wives shared an apartment at Lindell Towers, a luxurious residence one block from the Melbourne, where the players stayed. Sewell and Southworth even shared a closet, with each man keeping his clothes in his half, while both wives got a full closet apiece. Since the Browns and Cardinals never played at home at the same time, the arrangement made perfect economic sense. Now the question was who would occupy the suite for the World Series. Before the final game against the Yankees, Sewell wired Southworth about the arrangement. Southworth immediately telephoned his roommate and generously reassured him, "I don't want to go into any ifs with you. The Browns are going to win the pennant, so you go right ahead. I have rooms available at a hotel, and I'll just move in there when we return home, and we'll proceed just as if we were still out of town."

Then Southworth added, "Don't worry, you'll win it." The two men were such good friends that during the Series they drove home together after each game.

Sewell also wanted to invite his mother to the Series. Fortunately, another resident of Lindell Towers was out of town during October and offered his apartment for her use.

The morning after the Browns victory, the St. Louis Cardinals boarded a train in New York, where they had wrapped up the season, and headed back to St. Louis and their third straight World Series. Everyone was whooping it up, primed to do battle with their hometown rivals. "In fact, you wonder if the Browns themselves are as happy as the Cards," said *St. Louis Star-Times* reporter Ray J. Gillespie, who was on board with the pennant-winning National League champions. Southworth told Gillespie he thought the Browns were the best-balanced club in the American League, and was quoted as saying, "You can't pick out a weak spot, and you can't pick out an individual star on the Browns. One day it's McQuinn who breaks up your game. The next day it's Moore, then it's Stephens. Yesterday it was Laabs."

Also on board was Ford Frick, president of the National League, and an assortment of umpires, baseball writers, radio announcers, and VIPs. Everyone was discussing the big news that Danny Litwhiler, the Cardinals left fielder, had gone lame and might not be able to start against the Browns. With or without Litwhiler, the Cardinals would be a formidable opponent, having concluded their season with 101 victories, as opposed to the Browns' 89—the fewest ever by a pennant winner in the 154-game season.

The 1944 World Series marked only the seventh time that teams from the same city had played each other in the fall classic. The Chicago

White Sox and Chicago Cubs had faced off once, in 1906; and on six occasions—in 1921, 1922, 1923, 1936, 1937, and 1941—the Yankees had played either the New York Giants or the Brooklyn Dodgers. Newspapers had already dubbed the St. Louis event the "Streetcar Series" because Sportsman's Park sat on Grand Avenue, a major north-south streetcar thoroughfare that ran through the city's midsection.

Over the years, many of baseball's immortals had hit home runs in Sportsman's Park, including Hornsby, DiMaggio, and Gehrig. Babe Ruth once hit a home run completely over the roof and onto Grand Avenue. Yet none was as drama-packed, or as important, as the two that Chet Laabs, who had simply refused to give up, sailed over the fence on that unforgettable October afternoon.

Who Are Those Guys?

There was a saying about St. Louis, a city founded by French fur traders on the western bank of the Mississippi River in 1764, that almost every baseball fan knew and that still resonates in the collective consciousness of most locals: "First in shoes, first in booze, and last in the American League." The city was first in shoes back in the day when Brown Shoe and some 150 other shoe factories were headquartered there, and when the city's breweries included Anheuser-Busch, Falstaff, Griesedieck Bros., St. Vrain, Cherokee, Lemp, Bavarian, and about forty others.

All of the brewers except for Anheuser-Busch, the world's largest and the maker of Budweiser, are gone now. So also, but for Brown Shoe, are the shoe factories. Like the Browns baseball team, the breweries and factories were relics of an era when St. Louis was a major transportation hub, beginning in the 1850s with the rise of steamboat traffic and the later expansion of the railroad.

In 1904 St. Louis celebrated its preeminence as one of the country's most dynamic and populous cities with the Louisiana Purchase Exhibition, or World's Fair, which attracted more than twenty million people. At the fair, a gigantic Ferris wheel carried 1,440 people at a time, 40 in each of 36 cars, more than 250 feet up in the air. Most visitors also got their first look at such wonders as the automobile and electric lights, and here the hot dog, the ice cream cone, Jell-O, peanut butter, and iced tea were also introduced to the American palate.

After 1904 the city began to lose both its commerce and its industry as the country's population expanded westward. The steamboats, breweries, and shoe factories gradually disappeared. As late as 1944, owing in large part to World War II, more than 100,000 passengers a day were still passing through St. Louis's Union Station, at one time the largest and busiest passenger rail terminal in the world. But by the 1950s, with air travel growing in popularity, even this majestic architectural landmark fell into decline, and it was finally closed down in 1978.

The Browns came to St. Louis by way of Milwaukee, another largely German city known for its beer making, where they were called the Milwaukee Brewers. The Brewers had been charter members of the American League, but in 1901 they migrated a few hundred miles south and became the Browns, a name that evoked the glorious history of another ball team, the St. Louis Brown Stockings under the management of Chris von der Ahe. In their debut year, the Browns finished second. Several years of prosperity followed, but in 1916 owner Robert Hedges sold the team to Philip Ball, who had previously owned the St. Louis Terriers, of the defunct Federal League. By this time, the Browns had firmly distinguished themselves for their losing ways, finishing in the cellar fourteen times and seventh twelve times.

Ball was more bad news for the Browns, managing to sabotage their chances to finish first in the American League in one blunder after the other. If the Browns had a resident genius, it was a man named Branch Rickey, one of the most important figures in the history of American sports, who in 1947 was to integrate baseball when, as general manager of the Brooklyn Dodgers, he put Jackie Robinson on the roster. A former lackluster Browns player, Rickey managed the team from 1913 to 1915. His ego was just as big as Ball's, with the difference that few men of that time, or any time, understood the business of baseball half as well. Sensing an opening after Rickey's fractious relationship with Ball became common knowledge, the St. Louis Cardinals made Rickey an offer he could not refuse, and he jumped teams. Ball had made no effort to keep him, and Rickey, much to the detriment of the Browns, was to remain with the Cardinals until 1942, building the club into a powerhouse.

After stealing away Rickey, the Cardinals' new owner, Sam Breadon, began toying with Ball some more. In 1920, no doubt at Rickey's Machiavellian urging, Breadon brazenly asked Ball if the Cardinals could share digs with the Browns in the latter's stadium, Sportsman's Park. The Cardinals were homeless after Breadon sold off the team's own home grounds, Robison Field, and invested all the money from the sale into expanding the minor-league system. It was a genius of a move because that farm system—baseball's first, and created by none other than Rickey— eventually produced some of the star players that formed the Cardinals' legendary Gashouse Gang of 1934 and built the foundation that enabled

Branch Rickey, who managed the Browns from 1913 to 1915, later helped build the Cardinals into a powerhouse. (National Baseball Hall of Fame Library, Cooperstown NY. AP/Wide World Photos)

the Cardinals to win more World Series contests than any other team except for the New York Yankees. But in the meantime, Breadon's adroit move had left the Redbirds homeless. The ever-clueless Ball agreed to rent the stadium to his hometown rivals.

For one shining moment, it did look as though Ball knew what he was doing. In 1922 the Browns roster had some of the best players in their franchise history, including George Sisler, a future Hall of Famer, and three stellar outfielders: Ken Williams, "Baby Doll" Jacobson, and

Donald Barnes, the wealthy owner of an investment company, purchased the Browns in 1936. (National Baseball Hall of Fame Library, Cooperstown NY)

Jack Tobin. From 1919 to 1923, and again in 1925, that trio batted .300 or better. By 1926 Ball was still confidently predicting that St. Louis would be home to a World Series and that the Browns would play host. In anticipation of that happy event, he increased the capacity of his ballpark from 18,000 to 30,000, using the rent money from the Cardinals to help defray the cost.

Ball's prediction turned out to be partly true—there was a World Series in St. Louis in 1926, and it was played in the newly expanded Sportsman's Park, when the Cardinals upset the Yankees, 4 games to 3. Until that point, St. Louis had always been known as a "Browns town." After 1926 it became a "Cardinals town." Ball died in 1933, having lost more than $300,000 during his eighteen years as Browns owner.

Donald L. Barnes, the wealthy president of American Investment Company, a small-loan firm, became interested in the Browns in 1936. The original price tag for the team was $325,000, too much even for Barnes to come up with. So in a unique move, he received permission from the Missouri Securities Commission to sell stock in the team to the people of St. Louis for $5 per share. Barnes made a payment of $50,000, and in the end, with other contributions and the stock sales, the team was sold for $375,000. Barnes became team president, and the stadium, which still belonged to Ball's estate, was initially leased by the Browns. Later the Browns were able to purchase the property as well.

In 1936, the first year of the new ownership, the Browns drew only 80,922 fans. The downward spiral continued as the Browns compiled a 144-316 record from 1937 to 1939.

Even baseball's star players from other teams could not awaken Browns fans from their coma. In 1941, for example, when visiting players Ted Williams batted .406 for the Boston Red Sox and Joe DiMaggio of the Yankees hit in fifty-six straight games, Browns' attendance was fewer than 2,000 a game, for a total of 141,000. The Cardinals, in contrast, drew 646,000. St. Louis, at the time, was one of only four cities with teams in both leagues, along with Chicago, Philadelphia, and Boston, while New York had three teams. Part of the Browns' problem was that by the 1930s St. Louis was no longer a two-team market. The city had the smallest drawing territory of any big-league club. Using a hundred-mile radius as the rule of thumb, the population figures for the American League broke down this way:

St. Louis	2,610,000
Chicago	7,090,000
Detroit	4,341,000
Cleveland	4,301,000
Washington	3,968,000
Boston	6,118,000
Philadelphia (50-mile radius)	7,000,000
New York	21,151,000

Detroit, Cleveland, and Washington all had only one club, yet larger populations than St. Louis. Much of the outlying area in Missouri, Illinois, Iowa, and the southern border states Kentucky and Tennessee was rural, with a relatively small population. Most baseball fans in the region naturally gravitated to the winning Cardinals.

In 1940 Barnes and business manager Bill DeWitt felt the team needed a veteran catcher to help develop their pitching. While some players were proven hitters, the pitching staff was erratic. One promising pitcher after another had been brought up from the minors, only to fail to perform well on the mound. Shareholders were grumbling. At the same time, Barnes and DeWitt decided to hire a new manager, and drew up a blueprint of what they were looking for. They agreed that the new helmsman had to meet three requirements: he had to be familiar with the American League, know how to handle pitchers, and be able to get along with and supervise the players. They then decided that a catcher would most likely fit the bill, because a player in that position knew pitching more intimately than did players at other positions, and also acted as a kind of field general.

That was when someone with Luke Sewell's best interests in mind approached DeWitt and said, "Why don't you get Sewell? He's had the best record with pitchers at more places than one: Cleveland, Washington, Chicago, and then back at Cleveland again. I don't believe you'll be able to find a man with that good a record at so many different places."

James Luther "Luke" Sewell, a mild-mannered Alabamian, was one of three baseball brothers. Joe had played for Cleveland, and Tom for the Chicago Cubs. Luke had spent only seventeen days in the minors, and then the next nineteen years in the big leagues. Rare among ballplayers, he was also a college graduate, having received his degree from the University of Alabama in 1921. Even more unusual, he was an avid reader and had collaborated on a sports novel with the prophetic title *World Series*.

Sewell was a catcher and caught his first season as a regular for Tris Speaker's Cleveland Indians. For the first five years, he had been confined to the bullpen. "But those weren't wasted years," he later recalled. "I was busy studying baseball." One insight that Sewell had gained was that "you don't just *play* baseball; you play it *against* another team." He studied the weaknesses of opposing hitters and the tactics of opposing managers. But studying baseball was not the only thing he focused on. He also *hustled*. If he had not hustled, even as a bullpen player, Sewell later declared, "I would never have been able to accomplish anything."

In fact, he accomplished two unique feats. First, he is the only catcher in history to have caught three no-hit games. Second, he once tagged out two runners at home plate in the same play. In a game against the Yankees, Lou Gehrig had held up, thinking a fly ball would be caught. Dixie Walker closed up on him, and Sewell tagged out both when they tried to score.

Fortunately, Sewell's reputation as a hustling player with a passion for the game coincided with the crisis faced by the Browns management.

Sewell was at home in Akron, Ohio, one day when the phone rang. His wife answered and told him Alva Bradley, the owner of the Cleveland Indians, was on the line. Bradley told Sewell that Don Barnes, owner of the Browns, had asked for permission to talk to him about a job as manager. Sewell replied that he was not interested. He liked working for the Indians because that meant he could go home at night. Furthermore, he explained, he planned on retiring from baseball at the end of the next season. It was time, Sewell said, that he began thinking about his future, which he thought might lie in the "rubber industry" (he was a tire salesman in the off-season) and certainly not with a team as god-awful as the Browns.

Bradley urged him to talk to Barnes, just as a courtesy. When Sewell continued to resist, Bradley insisted. A few days later Sewell took a train to St. Louis. In his pocket was a plane ticket back to Cleveland, because in his mind he just wanted to get this favor to his boss over and done with.

Sewell later remembered that there was "a big gabfest" in Barnes's apartment between the Browns' owner, DeWitt, Howard Stevens (another Browns official), and himself. Trying to be cooperative, Sewell outlined his ideas about how a baseball team ought to be managed. He told them all the mistakes so many big-league managers made and emphasized in particular the subject of authority. "A manager," Sewell insisted, "*has* to be able to do what he *believes* with his players." He was laying it on thick because he still had no interest in the job and was just giving his hosts the benefit of his twenty years' worth of studying baseball.

Sewell also stressed the importance of giving the manager a long-term contract. He would need time, the catcher explained, to work out whatever situation he found himself in, and be solely responsible for the consequences. Sewell realized he was being not merely coldly objective but almost belligerent; he was genuinely not in the mood to take charge of a last-place team. He wanted to get out of baseball, and he was simply a downstairs guy venting to some upstairs people who, he assumed, probably correctly, did not understand baseball half as well as he did.

"That's very interesting," Barnes finally said when Sewell had terminated his monologue. "How much would you want to do all this for the Browns?"

Sewell threw out a figure.

"Will you let us have a few minutes?" Barnes said.

The three men filed out of the room. When they returned, Barnes said, "Well, you're the new manager of the Browns."

Sewell thought to himself: Wait a minute. Who made that decision, you or me? At the same time, he realized that it was probably a good decision. The rubber industry could wait—and he could also put all his theories into practice. He accepted the job.

Even so, despite the good money he had been offered, Sewell still thought of himself as a player. All that winter he worked at his other job. In the spring, he joined the Browns at their spring training camp in Florida.

What neither Sewell nor any of the players knew was that by the end of the 1941 season Barnes and his disgusted group of investors had decided to sell the team. Despite the hiring of a new manager, plans were drawn up to transfer the Browns to the West Coast. Barnes was enticed to move by a sweetheart deal offered by the Pacific Coast League's mainstay, Los Angeles, where the team would not only play in a new ballpark but be guaranteed half a million in annual ticket sales. In St. Louis, the Browns barely drew 150,000 fans annually. The move was to be officially endorsed at the annual meeting of major-league owners, to be held that year in Chicago on Monday, December 8.

But on Sunday morning, December 7, squadrons of Japanese Zeros bombed the American fleet at Pearl Harbor. As one sportswriter has remarked, "If the Japanese had attacked one day later, the St. Louis Browns' existence would have ceased at the end of '41. A great deal of craziness and wonderment, including a Browns pennant, would have been lost. Instead, Pearl Harbor prolonged the existence of the Browns franchise for another dozen years."

To their credit, the Browns owners then decided to spend some real money and compete seriously with their hometown rivals for attendance. After all, they had just hired a new manager who had some fancy ideas about believing and hustling. Perhaps Barnes decided it was time to do a little believing and hustling himself.

When Sewell arrived for his first spring training camp with the Browns, he found the situation about as bad as it could be. There was not a hint of team spirit, and the men had completely lost their will to win. Baseball, for most of the players, had become, not a game, but drudgery. The challenge was somehow to create a team that met three criteria: ability, superb physical condition, and that all-important desire to win.

Physical training, at the time, followed fairly conventional rules about exercising and running around a track. Sewell immediately introduced a few changes. The first required that the men rise early enough to eat in the camp dining room and be on the field by ten o'clock. Sewell knew from his winter job that men in the business world got up early—at seven, in Sewell's case—and were at work by nine. There seemed to be no good reason why baseball should be any different.

From the beginning, he was met with insubordination. Sewell had identified something he called the "second-division complex," and knew that most of his players were infected with it. They played ball just for the money. When Sewell gave them an inspirational talk, saying he thought they really could become a winning team, many of the men simply looked at him, as he later recalled, "with that innocent-sophisticated expression that said, 'Who do you think you're kiddin', bub?' "

On the very first day of the ten o'clock breakfast rule, a veteran player decided instead to take breakfast in his room at noon, along with some of his teammates. Sewell went to see him.

"Jeez," the player cried, "you're tryin' to run my private life; you're invadin' my personal rights."

"No, I'm not trying to run your private life," Sewell told him. "I'm trying to win ball games. That's my job. And you can't do it when you're not in condition."

The player gave him a dubious look and said, "Quit kiddin'."

Sewell informed him that from then on, there would be a $100 fine every time he failed to obey the rules.

After that, slowly and painfully, Sewell was gradually able to get his team into top physical condition and to instill in them the beginning of that vital will to win. He also decided that the best way to keep his players in line, and in shape, was to hire Bob Bauman, a no-nonsense trainer who during the winter months worked with student athletes at St. Louis University. He had never trained professionals before, and agreed to Sewell's proposal on one condition—that he convene the team and let Bauman talk to them. Sewell agreed, and the players were assembled.

Bauman told them, "Your manager has asked me to check you on the road, and I've accepted. I'm going to check you every night at 12 o'clock and I want you to be in your rooms. That's all I ask. I don't want any trouble about it. If you've got anything to say about it, say it now, because I don't want any trouble later on."

He was met with silence, which he took as consent. After that, Bauman never had any trouble, though on a few occasions, during his midnight checks, he would find Shirley in bed with his hat still on, or someone lying drunk under his bed.

On the road the players found other ways to entertain themselves. In Boston, for example, they were staying in rooms that faced a courtyard. With no air-conditioning, the windows were left open, and the players frequently hollered at each other across the court. A few had brought firecrackers, and as a practical joke would launch a cherry bomb onto guests passing through the courtyard below. With the war on, many people got quite frightened, and the hotel switchboard would light up.

Many of the players that Sewell found on his team, though they had previously played with other big-league clubs, had arrived at the Browns doorstep with less than enthusiastic recommendations from the scouts and farm clubs. The report on husky Vernon Stephens from the Browns' Toledo, Ohio, farm team, for example, noted that he put his foot in the basket, bailing out at the plate, could not hit a curveball, and could not field. Sewell watched him closely and saw Stephens strike out twice on curveballs. But he also hit two other pitches out of the park. Sewell knew that the Browns needed that kind of power. Even though Stephens continued to fan out during spring training, Sewell encouraged him to "keep swinging." In 1944 Sewell's confidence was to pay off, with Stephens leading the league in driving in runs with 109.

Sewell and his coaches also gave Stephens pointers on how to improve his fielding. A fielder who stands with his toes pointed out, they told him, is always resting on his heels and cannot get a jump on the ball. "Turn your toes so your feet are parallel and balance your weight on the balls of your feet," they advised him. By 1944 Stephens had become one of the best outfielders in the business.

What Sewell was looking for in his hitters was not stance or form. He understood that every hitter had what he called a "natural stroke" that was the consequence of his particular physical size, as well as his bone structure and muscular makeup. Trying to change that natural stroke, Sewell felt, was a waste of time, but that did not mean a natural stroke

Members of the St. Louis Browns—(from left) Mike Kreevich, Don Gutteridge, and Nelson Potter—celebrate after defeating the Yankees on the second-to-last day of the season. (National Baseball Hall of Fame Library, Cooperstown NY)

could not be trained to become a "base-hit stroke." Sewell worked on getting his batters to use their natural form to pound out base hits instead of flying deep into the outfield or bashing the ball into the dirt.

Sewell also wanted the team to be "strong down the middle," with a solid defense ranging along an axis from catcher to pitcher, second baseman, shortstop, and center fielder. When the team started to rebuild in 1942, after climbing from seventh place to a tie for sixth, the opportunity arose to obtain infielder Don Gutteridge from the Cardinals.

"Don't get him," Sewell was advised, "he's got bad hands."

But Sewell had seen Gutteridge play and thought he had a different problem. Instead of having bad hands, Gutteridge was not always accurate when he threw overhand from shortstop or third base, where he had been playing. Sewell decided that the best solution was to play Gutteridge at second, where he could throw sidearm. The result was that the new second baseman became, as Sewell later described him, "a leader and a spark plug for our team."

Sewell turned a number of other players who had been losers for other clubs into winners, and when asked about the secret of his success, he explained it this way: "I figure that there are smart baseball minds in every big-league organization. These players were brought up to the big league because some smart baseball man saw something of value in that particular player. Our approach, then, as soon as we got one of these men, was to try to find out what was the particular forte for which this player was brought up to the big leagues and then try to fit that special strength into our picture."

There was also the difficult, sometimes even insurmountable, problem of instilling assertiveness into a player. Sewell wanted his pitchers, in particular, to feel that they were the "boss" of a ball game out on the mound. That was what was holding back Denny Galehouse, Sewell felt. He thought Galehouse had the stuff necessary to be as great a pitcher as Burleigh Grimes, a star in the 1920s. Sewell got Galehouse to work on "developing a move to first." Without that skill, a pitcher was unable to work on a batter to the best of his ability because he was concentrating on the runner. That was how a game could be lost: the pitcher got into a jam, the batter got a hit, and the base runner scored. After Galehouse honed his first base throw, he developed, in Sewell's opinion, into one of the finest pitchers in baseball.

At the beginning of the season, Galehouse was employed with Good-year Aircraft in Akron, earning between $9,000 and $10,000 a year and putting in up to seventy hours in a six-day week. During his lunch break, he worked out, if he could find a fellow employee to serve as a catcher for him. After he signed on with the Browns as a Sunday pitcher, he would catch a train on weekends to whatever city the Browns were playing in, arrive early in the morning, have breakfast, and then go to the ballpark. Sunday doubleheaders were the order of the day, and Galehouse would always pitch the first game, then head for the showers and catch a train back home.

The strain soon began to show. At first, though he did not win any games, Galehouse was able to keep the runs scored by the other team to a minimum. The problem was, as he later recalled, "From a pitching standpoint, the hitters were a little bit easier to pitch to than prior to World War II. But then the fielders weren't quite as good, so it would kind of balance."

Galehouse was also getting out of shape. Finally, he decided he had to make up his mind and choose between baseball and the war plant. He took a trip to Sarasota, Florida, where he had lived during the registration period for the draft, and asked the draft board, "Now, I am considering quitting the war job, because it looks like we've got a chance to win the pennant. How long would I have before I'm taken into the service?" The draft board replied, "You probably wouldn't take your physical before the end of the season." Galehouse decided to take the chance, quit his job, and played full-time. He was finally drafted in April 1945.

Galehouse was one of Sewell's success stories, but the Browns' new manager was not always able to instill new skills and attitudes in his players. Sewell tried hard to get one pitcher to throw a curve, and showed him how it was done. The man worked on his new pitch for just two days, then gave up. Sewell instantly dropped him from the team. Another player, a catcher, had the bad habit of always signaling for a certain pitch in the clutch. Eventually, word about his predictability spread among rival teams, who took full advantage of it. Sewell let him go as well.

Every player on the Browns team was looked upon as an individual and treated differently. Pitcher Nelson Potter had a weak knee, so Sewell made sure he got plenty of rest. Sewell also understood the virtue of patience, and that trying to get results too quickly only led to confusion.

Another Sewell rule was to guard against forming friendships with his men. Much as he may have admired them, some more than others, he also knew that it was difficult to look on a friend with a cold, objective eye. Players, Sewell believed, were "material," and there were always problems with this material; a manager's job was to examine his material, identify the problem, and then fix it, regardless of the consequences.

For the 1942 season, the team finished with a whopping (for the Browns) attendance record of 255,617 and an 82-69 record, a .543 percentage, which was the fourth loftiest in the team's pennantless forty-year history. However, after finishing a respectable third in 1942, the Browns slipped back to sixth place in 1943 with a disappointing 72-80 mark.

Despite the rebuilding of the team, the Browns in 1944 were still a motley collection of castoffs, rookies, and misfits at best, and a bit demented at worst. Perhaps the Browns' greatest good fortune was having the Selective Service System declare first baseman McQuinn and short-stop Stephens unfit for service after they flunked their physicals. In the six World Series games, McQuinn was to bat .438 and hit the Browns' only homer in Series history.

Stephens was a typical Browns player. His roommate during the regular season was Galehouse, who recalled, "You'd wake up in the morning, and his bag would be there at the foot of the bed, wouldn't even be opened. The bed wouldn't be touched. And women—every gal who looked at him wanted to hop in bed with him. He had three names, Vern, Stevie, and Junior, and the phone would ring all night. Nobody would put up with that all night for very long. 'Is Vern there?' 'No, he ain't here.' 'Is Stevie there?' 'Is Junior there?' "

The unforgettable 1944 season began inauspiciously on March 19 when one Browns catcher and four pitchers filed off a train at Cape Girardeau, Missouri, and were met by eight members of the Cape Girardeau Baseball Committee chaired by Mayor Ray Beckman. Spring training officially began the next day, and by then nine players were on hand. Temperatures were below freezing.

The Browns were now training in Cape Girardeau, an old French settlement on the Mississippi River, because of new war rules that major-league teams had to train more or less within a hundred miles of their home city. The main reason was not so much security as to reduce civilian traffic on the overburdened railroads, which were now responsible for transporting literally millions of service personnel around the country.

While waiting for the weather to turn warm, the Browns and their top farm club, the Toledo Mudhens, trained in Southeast Missouri State Teachers College's arena, which was built for horse shows and had a dirt floor—ideal for infield practice. They also practiced at a nearby abandoned sandstone quarry that was protected from the wind and had a running track. In the college gymnasium, Sewell turned up the thermostat so that his players would perspire and get acclimatized to the hot summer days ahead.

Other members of the Browns eventually trickled in, including Mike Kreevich, who said his ailing leg had been strengthened by his winter job as a milkman. Kreevich had been released by the Athletics after the 1942 season because he drank too much. But Sewell had played with Kreevich on the Chicago White Sox in the late thirties and thought he was worth claiming. A few months earlier, Sewell had gone to Springfield, Illinois, where Kreevich lived, and met him at the Abraham Lincoln Hotel on a wintry Sunday morning. Kreevich staggered in.

"Mike, we can use you," Sewell told him, "but only if you're sober. If you don't stay sober I'm going to have to release you."

"You don't have to worry about it," Kreevich assured him.

"How much do you want?" Sewell asked.

When Kreevich named a figure, Sewell said, "Now, I'm going to give you another $2,000."

That brought Kreevich's salary to $14,000. Later, Sewell contacted a friend of his, someone he once described as "one of the originators of Alcoholics Anonymous," and asked him to get someone to help Kreevich down in Springfield. One day a group of men came to the hotel to talk to the center fielder, though with what result is not known.

Kreevich, who had a draft deferment because his two children had been born before the bombing of Pearl Harbor, was a devout Catholic. DeWitt arranged with Kreevich's brother to have a local priest stop in from time to time to see how Kreevich was getting along. The Browns also roomed him with Don Gutteridge, a nondrinker, who always made sure the hotel dresser was stacked with candy bars.

On the other hand, three of the Browns players, including McQuinn, were ex-seminarians. They never went out drinking and spent their evenings away sitting in the hotel lobby, waiting for their teammates to return from the bars all skinned up and bloody. McQuinn was married to Kathleen Baker McQuinn, a tall, dark-haired woman from Belfast, Ireland. They had met on a blind date at a baseball game, the first one she had ever seen, while he was playing minor-league ball in Toronto. Off season, the McQuinns lived in Alexandria, Virginia, where he managed a movie theater.

Mark Christman lived in the nearby St. Louis suburb of Kirkwood, and his wife, Virginia, often took a bus and a streetcar to get to the ballpark, if she could find a babysitter for their two children. They had met at a high school in Maplewood, another suburb.

Nelson Potter, a screwball pitcher, had won nineteen games for a minor-league team in Louisville in 1942, but was considered a has-been by most major-league clubs. In 1938 Potter, who was suffering from a torn cartilage in his right knee, underwent an operation in Philadelphia. The surgeon compounded Potter's woes by removing the wrong cartilage. Two years later, as a member of the Boston Red Sox, he underwent a second operation, this time in Chicago. Though the knee repair was successful this time around, Potter failed to improve on the mound and was sent to Louisville, who sold him to the Browns in 1943.

While throwing for the Browns, Potter practiced developing a slider. Before that, he had relied mainly on his screwball and a curveball, since his fastball was never too impressive. Batters leaning out over the plate, expecting the screwball, soon found a slider sailing past their wrists. As a

After Chet Laabs left his war-plant job and began playing for the team full-time, he became a major factor in St. Louis's winning the American League pennant. (National Baseball Hall of Fame Library, Cooperstown NY)

result, Potter became one of the Browns' most productive pitchers. Few pitchers at the time even threw a slider, which was a pitch that broke hard away from hitters, with much more velocity than a curveball.

During the 1943 season, the Browns also obtained third baseman Ellis Clary in a trade for Harlond Clift with Washington. Sewell was determined to rid the team of players like Clift, who had a losing attitude. Though Clary was a popular player because of his wit, he also had a reputation for precipitating fights. "Clary was real good with his fists," recalled his teammate Red Hayworth. "He was a street fighter. He was a fellow who could smile and hit you at the same time." While waiting for Clary to arrive from Washington, though, Sewell put utility player Christman at third; and by the time Clary arrived in St. Louis two weeks later, the job was taken.

In casting about for pitching help, DeWitt signed up two long shots. One was Alvis "Tex" Shirley, twenty-six, of Birthright, Texas, who had been released by the Athletics after losing his only decision in 1942. Shirley drank a lot and had a temper. The other, Jakucki, drank even more and had a worse temper.

Sig Jakucki was more accomplished as a drinker and a brawler than as a ballplayer when he joined the Browns in 1944. (National Baseball Hall of Fame Library, Cooperstown NY)

When the 1944 season began, Galehouse and Laabs were still tied to war-plant jobs in Akron and Detroit, respectively; relief pitcher Bob Muncrief had a war-plant job in Houston; Potter, expecting to be drafted after undergoing his physical examination, was in Chicago. Others who had war-plant jobs included outfielders Mike Shartak and Al Zarilla and infielder Mark Christman. They played on weekends when they could. Other 4-F players were catcher Angelo Giuliani and pitcher Earl Jones. Even so, some Browns players were demanding raises, perhaps inspired by word that pitcher Mort Cooper of the Cardinals was asking for a salary increase of $5,500. "Why, one of our players with nothing but Class AA experience has asked for a salary that we would pay a regular after four or five years in the majors," Bill DeWitt complained to the *Sporting News*.

Sig Jakucki, the big ex-soldier who had last pitched in the majors in 1936 and then drank and slugged his way around the minors, got into his first brawl on the very day he showed up at the Browns' training camp in Cape Girardeau. The entire Browns team had gone to a bar, and Jakucki was half-sloshed when Shirley, a bald, abrasive, Stetson-wearing Texan, got impatient that his beers were not coming fast enough. Shirley, sensitive about his premature baldness, always wore a cowboy hat. "When he was forced to remove his hat in hotel dining rooms and other proper establishments, a teammate once recalled, his white pate stood out against his suntanned face like snow on a mountaintop." Shirley decided to take out his frustration on Jakucki by giving the new arrival a "beer shampoo." Jakucki, who got into fights at the drop of a Stetson himself, hit Shirley "right in the mouth and damn near knocked the wall down with him," recalled Clary. "Tex's mouth the next morning looked like a freight train had run through it."

One of the most unusual ballplayers of all time, a rough-and-tumble veteran who had rambled around the world playing semipro ball, Jakucki had been born in Camden, New Jersey, on August 20, 1909. In 1927 he joined the army. Sent to Honolulu, he played baseball for the army base team. He proved to be such an outstanding player that a local promoter allegedly paid the military to release Jakucki, who was then serving his second term. Whether or not the rumors were true, the army did grant Jakucki an early medical discharge that enabled him to pursue a career in baseball.

Jakucki made his debut in the minors as a shortstop, an outfielder, and an occasional pitcher for the Honolulu Braves. He got his first taste of playing in the majors when an All-Star team that included Jakucki's hero,

Al Simmons, as well as Lou Gehrig, Frankie Frisch, Mickey Cochrane, Lefty O'Doul, and Lefty Grove, was touring in the off-season and played the Braves. The fans loved Jakucki not only as a colorful personality but also as a phenomenal hitter. He was eventually offered to the San Francisco Seals, a minor-league outfit with greater visibility, but that team already had the young Joe DiMaggio in the outfield and decided to pass. Instead, Jakucki went across the bay and was signed up by the Oakland Oaks of the Pacific Coast League. He soon discovered, though, that in trying to hold his own, much less excel, he was outclassed. Playing in the boondocks of Hawaii was one thing; competing in a top-level minor-league team in California another. The Oaks released him in May.

Eventually, Jakucki wound up in Galveston, where he was signed up by the Sand Crabs, a shipyard team that played in the Texas League. The team's manager, Bill Webb, convinced him that the only way he could continue to play professional ball and one day make it into the majors was to stop playing outfield and become a full-time pitcher. Jakucki took the advice, and in 1934 posted a 10-7 record for the Sand Crabs. The following season he pitched a no-hitter while compiling a 15-14 record and pitching 51 games, the most in the league.

During a game in June 1936, Jakucki's famed temper revealed itself on the field when he climbed into the stands in Houston to throw a punch at a spectator. Though he was suspended, he still managed to pitch a seven-inning no-hitter (in the minor leagues, games in doubleheaders were limited to seven innings). Soon after that performance, the Browns bought Jakucki from Galveston. During spring training in 1937, though he made the team, he never appeared in a game, and he was eventually sent back to Texas. Later that year he pitched for the New Orleans Pelicans.

According to Arthur Daley in the *New York Times*, Jakucki and Pelicans manager Euel Moore once went to see a wrestling match after a game. The hefty, playful Moore had the reputation of being the strongest man in baseball, and in Jakucki he found a kindred soul. The wrestling match turned out to be slightly on the boring side, so to provide some excitement Moore "picked up the 200-pound Sig," Daley wrote, "and tossed him into the ring. The startled grapplers thought Jakucki was merely part of the act and that someone had forgotten to tip them off. But the indignant referee took a swing at Jakucki, a sad mistake." Jakucki flattened him. "Thereupon the two wrestlers pounced on the interloper, also a mistake." Moore joined in until the police broke up the free-for-all and carted Jakucki and Moore to the nearest jail. When someone phoned Larry Gilbert, owner of the Pelicans, to inform him that his two wildest birds were in the clink and to ask for instructions on what to do, he replied without hesitation, "Leave them there. Then I'll at least know where they are."

At the end of the season, Jakucki gave up professional baseball. Succumbing to wanderlust, he spent the next few years hoboing around the globe, traveling to China and the Philippines.

During World War II, most major-league ballplayers in the military did not serve overseas but were recruited to play stateside for their camp team. Early in 1944, Jakucki was recruited to pitch against an army camp team in Texas led by Sid Hudson, a pitcher for the Washington Senators who had won forty games in his first three seasons before entering the service. Jakucki's performance in that game impressed both the Browns management and that of the New York Giants, and both teams contacted him. Good players, after all, were now scarce. Jakucki chose his former team, the Browns, who thought they were getting a thirty-one-year-old pitcher who gave his birth date as 1912, not 1909. During his first stint as a Brownie, he had listed 1911 as his birth date.

Browns vice president Bill DeWitt later told the *Sporting News* how the team recruited Jakucki:

> A player who had been with us, and was working in the Galveston shipyards, sent me word that a pitcher named Jakucki down there was showing enough stuff to warrant the belief he could win in the American League. I knew something about Jakucki. We had paid $12,500 for Jakucki to Shreveport [in fact, Galveston], and had released him after the training season. I wrote for more dope on the pitcher. My correspondent insisted Jakucki could win in the American League, not only this year, but in the circuit as it was before the war. I finally sent for Jakucki. Look at him now—the man who will win the pennant for us, the greatest bargain in the history of the big leagues.

It was a brave statement on DeWitt's part, since Jakucki had not pitched in the majors for eight years when the Browns signed him, and had in fact never won a single game in the majors. Nor did DeWitt or Sewell have any real grasp of Jakucki's drinking and personality problems. Jakucki demanded a clause in his contract that he be rewarded for each win over ten. Baseball rules at the time prohibited any bonus based on accomplishments and allowed only those based on attendance, so the request was denied. Even so, Jakucki boasted that he would win between twelve and fifteen games that season, and on September 26 he would post his twelfth victory in a 1 to 0 win over Boston. During the season Jakucki had found a unique way to improve his game by holding a four-pound metal ball in his hand for up to a quarter of an hour before a game. By game time, the actual baseball felt as light as a tennis ball.

Gutteridge, who taught junior high school in Pittsburgh, Kansas, had wired that he would be arriving late to training camp. When he did show up, he was accompanied by fourteen-year-old Ted Atkinson, the son of Billy Atkinson, a onetime middleweight boxing figure. Perhaps Ted Atkinson, who had hoped to make the team as an outfielder, was inspired by the story of James Eugene Richardson, who stood six feet tall when he enlisted in the Navy at age fourteen. Richardson was dispatched to the Gilbert Islands, where his ruse was discovered and he was sent home. So was Atkinson.

Catcher Frank Mancuso, fresh out of the army, arrived for spring training in his soldier's uniform. He had injured his back during a parachute drill in the Pacific and been sent home. Mancuso was fit enough to play for the Browns in 1944, but his injury caused a unique problem for a catcher—he could not look up for a pop-up. If Mancuso looked up, the sudden movement would cut off the oxygen to his brain and he would pass out. Instead, when a batter lofted a fly directly over the plate, or in foul territory, the first baseman, third baseman, and pitcher would charge in to make a play on it. But Mancuso's injury went unnoticed by opponents and, remarkably, never cost the Browns an out. Mancuso, who had played with the Browns' San Antonio farm team in 1942, shared the catching duties with Red Hayworth in 1944.

Another player Sewell brought up was Milt "Skippy" Byrnes, an outfielder from Toledo, who was 4-F because of a bronchial condition. He also had difficulty judging fly balls. Yet Browns scouting was so faulty that the report on him when he was in the minors said that he was one of the better center fielders but could not hit. "We found it was just reversed," Sewell later recalled. "He was a good hitter but couldn't field."

Sewell's pitching staff before spring training included five southpaws: Al Hollingsworth, Sam Zoldak, Virgil Brown, Waldon West, and Raymond Campbell. By March 24, though, more than ten players had still not reported, and the DeWitt brothers (Bill's brother Charlie was the co-owner of the team) were clearly worried. In practice games against the Mudhens, pitchers were filling both outfield and infield spots. Two were

If Browns catcher Frank Mancuso looked up while trying to catch a pop-up, the oxygen would cut off to his brain and he would pass out. (National Baseball Hall of Fame Library, Cooperstown NY)

definite holdouts—Byrnes and pitcher Jack Kramer, who had received a medical discharge from the army. Eight others remained unsigned as well. The Cape Girardeau newspaper reported that they were holding out for an average $500 a year increase in pay.

The weather was so drizzly and cold that March, down in southern Missouri, that both Hollingsworth and Potter wound up in the hospital with the flu, while several other players suffering from bad sore throats were confined to their rooms.

One night Sewell went searching for his players and found Kreevich—who had promised his manager that his drinking would not become a problem—sitting in a bar.

"Mike, you've had enough," Sewell told him.

Both men returned to the hotel. Sewell locked his player in the room and pocketed the key. A half hour later, he decided to make another round, walked back to the same bar, and found Mike sitting on the same stool. Kreevich had exited his room via a window that opened onto the fire escape.

Another concern was the virtue of the town's young women. At the start of spring training, the mayor and the head of the Chamber of Commerce told Bill DeWitt, "You know, this is a small town, and a very religious town, and there's a lot of gossip."

Obligingly, Jakucki told the *Sporting News* that his playboy days were behind him and that he was confident he would make the team. However, insofar as he, Shirley, Kreevich, and a few other hard drinkers had lost no time finding the best bars in town, including one that was in the back room of a drugstore, it seems reasonable to assume they also went looking for female companionship wherever they could find it, with no regard for any assurances made on their behalf by Browns management.

The Browns broke camp on April 8 and traveled to St. Louis for a "City Series" of six exhibition games against the Cardinals. Sewell and Bill DeWitt took a train back to St. Louis, while the coaches and players rode back in a bus. In that preseason preview of the World Series, the Browns won only one of the half dozen intercity games.

Meanwhile, of course, there was still a war going on. On April 16 General Douglas MacArthur issued a statement in response to reports that the Republican Party might draft him to run for president. "I have not sought the office nor do I seek it," he said. "My sole ambition is to assist our country to win this vital struggle by the fulfillment of such duty as has been, or may be, assigned to me." The rationing of lard ended.

A Lutheran army chaplain at Fort McClellan, Arkansas, reported that German war prisoners being held there were in good spirits and that their favorite songs were "Pistol Packin' Momma" and "Mairzy Doats," both of which were on the top of the Hit Parade.

By the end of spring training, a few players had still not signed contracts. These men were not holding out for a raise, however, but simply waiting to be inducted. Both McQuinn and Stephens had been tentatively reclassified 1-A. Yet when they were called to take their physicals once again, they both flunked a second time. Tex Shirley was inducted, examined, and rejected seven times; he had a hernia.

Adding to the uncertainty was the very nature of the Selective Service System. In December 1943 General Lewis B. Hershey, the director of Selective Service, had estimated that two million men needed to be drafted by July of the following year. On February 26, 1944, President Roosevelt criticized the Selective Service for "over leniency" in granting occupational deferments, saying there was a "grave shortage" of manpower for the armed forces. Hershey barred occupational deferments for men twenty-six or younger except in critical cases. But local draft boards interpreted that edict according to local conditions. "A Wisconsin board deferred 24 young men as vital to the cheese industry."

Then, in April 1944, the military abruptly suspended the induction of draftees twenty-seven or older. Unexpectedly, a group of men who had begun to bid their families an emotional farewell and to make elaborate preparations for departure suddenly found themselves with nowhere to go. The navy agreed to take these men so that their leave-takings would not go to waste.

At the start of the 1944 season, an optimistic mood had begun to take root in the country. In Detroit, the General Motors Corporation announced that it would spend $500 million to reconvert its factories for car production after the war, and predicted a boom in automobile sales. In Washington, the House Ways and Means Committee imposed new taxes, including an increase from 10 percent to 20 percent in the admission tax on baseball tickets. In New York's Times Square, the theater district was once again ablaze with lights. The *New York Times* reported that New Year's Eve celebrations were in marked contrast to those of the year before, adding, "The whole picture seemed to have changed since then, from dark foreboding to the certainty of victory."

The 1944 season also marked a showdown of a different sort for the two St. Louis clubs, and both Bill DeWitt and Breadon made no secret of the fact that either the Cardinals or the Browns would have to leave town. "St. Louis can no more support two major league clubs than Kansas City could support one," Breadon said.

Other baseball owners saw different problems lying in the future. Alva Bradley, owner of the Indians, thought professional baseball ought to close down for the duration of the war, rather than offer fans a substandard game. Branch Rickey, now the general manager of the Brooklyn Dodgers, warned that baseball was in danger of losing its honored place in the hearts of Americans. "Baseball must take heed, or football will become our national sport," he said. His prescient warning was ignored. Football at the time attracted so little attention that the *Sporting News* had not even begun to cover it until the fall of 1942.

Rickey was worried about baseball's future mainly because of the deterioration of the minor leagues. In 1940, at the peak of the minor-league system, there were forty-three leagues with teams in 314 cities. Three years later, the draft had so dried up the supply of players that only nine minor leagues were able to function, with a total of sixty-two teams. Rickey suggested that, after the war, about seventy-five minor leagues be established to preserve baseball's preeminence in sport. What he could not foresee, of course, was a technological development "that would have an even more devastating impact on minor league baseball than a world war, and would greatly enhance the popularity of professional football: television."

Another suggestion to save baseball fell on deaf ears. During the winter of 1943–44 a delegation of blacks, headed by the singer Paul Robeson, met with baseball commissioner Kenesaw Mountain Landis and the team owners during their annual meeting. Robeson suggested that black players be allowed to play in organized baseball. Only a few months earlier, the Negro Giants had defeated a team of major- and minor-league stars in an exhibition game 4 to 3, with Satchel Paige striking out fourteen batters. Robeson was told that the American public would never tolerate such a thing.

In Sportsman's Park blacks had to sit in the right field pavilion, where they viewed the game through a screen that stretched from the outfield wall to the roof above. The segregation of fans ended only after the 1944 season, when Sportsman's Park became the last professional ballpark to end the practice. Ballplayers and sportswriters often joked that St. Louis and Washington were the two "Confederate" cities on the league circuit.

Ironically, when German prisoners of war were shipped by train across the American South, they sat in first-class seats. Black soldiers, in contrast, while wearing their uniforms, medals, and combat ribbons, sat in their customary second-class seats in the back of the train.

The 1944 Browns team that Sewell put on the field on the first day of the season was not much different from the 1943 team. The two most significant changes he had made involved catchers Hayworth and Mancuso, who started slowly in the spring but gradually gained self-confidence. What Sewell most wanted to guard against was a replay of a situation in 1943 when the Browns were standing three games in front when they played a series against the Yankees. In the first game an umpire's decision went against the St. Louis team, which promptly lost spirit, went into a tailspin, lost the entire series, and soon found itself in sixth place.

As one sportswriter noted, the Browns' pitching staff and outfield "had the appearance of something discarded by the Salvation Army." Another writer opined that the Browns were "the strangest group of athletes ever assembled on one club." The Browns' perpetual lock on last place was such a national joke that even Hollywood took note of it. In May 1944 the movie *Going My Way* premiered. In one scene, crooner Bing Crosby, playing a sports-loving priest, appears in the basement of a church rectory wearing a Browns cap and jacket. "Always in the cellar," someone quips.

Many of the men in the Browns lineup were old for baseball players. McQuinn and Jakucki were thirty-five, Gutteridge thirty-two, Christman thirty, Kreevich thirty-six, Moore thirty-four, Laabs thirty-two. Both Hollingsworth and Caster were thirty-six, Steve Sundra thirty-four, Potter and Galehouse thirty-two, and Muncrief twenty-eight. Byrnes, at twenty-seven, was among the youngest.

The Browns also led the major league in 4-F players, starting the season with eighteen 4-Fs, and thirteen made the squad for the long run: McQuinn, first base; Gutteridge, second base; Stephens, shortstop; Clary and Floyd Baker, utility infield; Milt Byrnes, outfield; Hayworth, catcher; and pitchers Kramer, Hollingsworth, Jakucki, Potter, Shirley, and Sam Zoldak. And catcher Mancuso had received an honorable discharge after being injured. The Browns' strength, the experts wryly concluded, "was in superior weakness." "Luke Sewell could put a pretty fair 4-F team on the field," observed the *Sporting News*.

But the Browns were not the only team with an abundance of 4-F players. The New York Giants, who finished last in 1943, opened the 1944 season with sixteen 4-F players, tops in the National League, and won their first five games. "The Giants now are almost as well fixed with men with creaky backs, twisted knees, and other rejection ailments as the Browns," the *Sporting News* reported. Publisher J. G. Taylor Spink said things had come to a terrible state "when pennant chances are rated in direct proportion to the number of physically handicapped performers retained by the various clubs."

At that very moment members of Congress were asking whether men with a 4-F status ought to be drafted for either military labor or war-plant jobs. The *Sporting News* pleaded with Congress not to enact such a drastic law. "Would it be against the best interests of this nation to appeal to Washington to let our 4-F players remain in the major leagues, where they could do America the most good, doing the thing they do best?" Fortunately, the legislation did not pass.

The scarcity of ballplayers was so severe that the *Sporting News* even proposed in an editorial that baseball players, like those employed in essential industries, should receive an occupational deferment. The government ignored the suggestion.

The Yankees, in particular, had lost numerous players to the war: Marius Russo and Roy Weatherly were inducted; Billy Johnson and Charlie Keller joined the Merchant Marines. Bill Dickey was drafted in the spring of 1944, and two days later so was Joe Gordon. They lost every starter of their 1942 championship team, including four catchers: Dickey, Aaron Robinson, Ken Sears, and Ken Silvestri. Red Rolfe, the star third baseman, had retired, and his stand-ins, Hank Majeski and Bill Johnson, were drafted. Five Yankee outfielders were in the service—DiMaggio, Tommy Henrich, Keller, Selkirk, and Weatherly. So were starting pitchers Red Ruffing and Marius Russo.

Other players the Yankees lost to the armed services or to essential industry included Spud Chandler, Johnny Murphy, Rollie Helmsley, and Frankie Crosetti. With such depletion in the ranks, speculation was rife among sportswriters that the Yankees could not possibly win a fourth straight pennant. Some thought they might even finish in the second division for the first time since 1925, which, in fact, they did, winding up in sixth place after losing the four straight to the Browns.

By the start of the 1944 season, 340 major-league players and more than 3,000 from the minor leagues were in military service. Yet not a single player of any reputation from the Browns between the 1943 and 1944 season was inducted. Most were deferred, 4-F, or ineligible for other reasons.

Sewell had high hopes for his pitchers Potter and Kramer, who had been brought back from Toledo. Al Hollingsworth had labored in the National League for years, but back in 1940 even the worthless Senators had shown him the exit. George Caster was another American League castoff, though he was proving to be good in relief; and Tex Shirley, up from Springfield, Massachusetts, of the Eastern League, was for all practical purposes a rookie. Galehouse was holding on to his war job and was available only for weekend pitching chores. Al Milnar left a real gap in the pitching staff, though, when the army took him.

But in a bizarre twist, Jakucki would turn out to be the real sensation of the season. During one thirty-seven-inning stretch, he gave up only one run, had three shutouts, and lost only one game—a 1 to 0 game against the Yankees in New York.

The strong infield was led by Stephens at shortstop, who by September was leading the league in runs batted in and fielding well ahead of his previous record. The reliable McQuinn held down first; Gutteridge played reasonably well at second; and Christman was doing a sensational job at third and was credited with providing the spark that kept the Browns' hopes alive.

In the outfield were Mike Chartak, Kreevich, Gene Moore, and Laabs, all refugees from other chain gangs in baseball and none regarded very highly by sportswriters or knowledgeable fans. But Milt Byrnes was batting well, and Zarilla, up from Toledo, had a hitting streak in July when he pounded out fifteen hits in eighteen times at bat, many of them for extra bases.

If the Browns had an Achilles' heel, it was their catching department. After Rick Ferrell was sold to Washington, Sewell was hoping that the unproven Hank Helf could take his place, but the army drafted him and that was that. Hayworth, brother of the more famous Ray, and Mancuso, brother of the great Gus, were given the responsibilities instead.

At the start of the 1944 season, sportswriters made their usual predictions. Jack Hand, of the Associated Press, named the New York Yankees, Washington Senators, and Chicago White Sox as preseason favorites, and put the Browns in last place. Martin J. Haley, of the *St. Louis Globe-Democrat*, picked the Cardinals to win their third straight National League pennant. The only positive thing he had to say about the Browns was that it was their forty-third straight season in the American League.

The only sports columnist who did pick the Browns at the start of the season was John F. Box, who wrote for the *Echo*, published by the

Huntsville, Texas, prison. "We urge you to step up and grab a ticket on the St. Louis Browns to cop the American League pennant," he wrote. "If their pitching holds up, the Browns are in. DeWitt's club has a keen competitive spirit. There are three facts in sports history that even Jimmy Durante will acknowledge: 1) Regret was the only filly ever to win the Kentucky Derby. 2) Dempsey got a long count. 3) The Browns never won a pennant. The last item is about to be corrected."

In the Browns' season opener at Detroit on April 17, Sewell picked Jack Kramer, who outdueled Dizzy Trout 2 to 1. The Browns won the next two games as well, and then headed home to play the Chicago White Sox for the home opener. The Coast Guard provided the band, the Navy Spars Drum and Bugle Corps marched, and Mayor Aloys P. Kaufmann threw out the first ball. "He had plenty of room for his windup, only 3,395 fans having come, including a thousand servicemen and children who got in free." Sewell took a chance and started Potter, who had not pitched a single inning during the exhibition season because of his illness. Kreevich, who had hit only one home run during the past three seasons, smacked a three-run homer in the first inning, and followed that one up with another. The Browns won 5 to 3.

On April 24, after the Browns had won four straight victories, General MacArthur announced that his forces had trapped 140,000 Japanese soldiers on islands stretching from the Solomons to New Guinea. "Time and combat will be required to accomplish their annihilation, but their ultimate fate is now certain. Their situation reverses Bataan." The United States and Britain also launched a nonstop air assault against Germany in preparation for the invasion of the European continent.

The Browns next swept a doubleheader from the White Sox, 5 to 2 and 4 to 3, extending their streak to six games and approaching to within one game of the American League record for consecutive victories at the start of the season, set by the 1933 Yankees. The doubleheader drew 7,709 paid fans, a huge crowd by Browns standards. During a two-day lull, the Browns got more good news when the Selective Service System permitted pitcher Bob Muncrief to leave his job at the Brown Shipbuilding Company in Houston and join the team. At the same time Spud Chandler, the Yankees' best pitcher, who had won twenty games in 1943, was drafted.

Commenting on the Browns' best start in forty-three years, *St. Louis Post-Dispatch* sportswriter W. J. Cogan reported in late April, "Those are strange expressions you see on the faces of followers of the Browns today as they stagger around in a daze thinking of the club's six-game winning streak which has put them in front in this young American League race."

In London, General George S. Patton told an audience that it was the destiny of the British and Americans "to rule the world, and the more we see of each other the better." Estimating the numbers killed at 177,000, he said he had been busy "welcoming Germans and Italians into hell" and hoped he would soon "have a chance to go and kill the Japanese."

The next day, the Browns tied the record by beating Cleveland 5 to 2, with Steve Sundra outpitching Allie Reynolds. Though the game was played in St. Louis, a mere 960 paying fans showed up. The next day, Potter pitched the record breaker, beating the Indians 5 to 1. "It may be stranger than fiction," wrote the *St. Louis Globe-Democrat*, "but it is a fact nevertheless—the St. Louis Browns have deprived the famed New York Yankees of one of their many records."

Finally, the Browns had begun to believe their manager that a pennant win was possible. "We realized that DiMaggio and Williams and all the rest of the big stars were off in the service," McQuinn later recalled. "We were just as good as anybody else." Even more amazing, the Browns had achieved their mighty feat on the strength of their pitching, which was supposedly their weak point. Shirley, despite his occasional wildness, was now showing particular promise.

After the game, for the first time in any player's memory, photographers crowded into the locker room, snapping pictures while reporters peppered the players with questions. Accustomed to dressing in heavy silence, the Browns suddenly were finding themselves the center of attention, cutting up and enjoying themselves. Quipped Gutteridge, "We only have to win 146 more to finish the season without a loss!"

The Cardinals had also got off to a great start that season, leading another *Post-Dispatch* columnist to wonder, as early as mid-April, "if our facetious selection of the two St. Louis clubs to meet in next October's World Series is still just a joke." The sportswriters and players were not the only ones excited by the Browns' good showing. The stock in the publicly traded company that owned the team continued to rise, advancing from $3.50 to $3.75 a share; at the opening of the season, the stock had traded at $1.50. According to brokers, the increase was the result of interest from new shareholders and not trading by a major shareholder or a pool.

Even so, on the day that the Browns set the American League record by winning their ninth straight win, fans were still neither convinced that the Browns were truly serious about changing their losing ways nor apparently much interested in seeing them establish a new record. Only 894 paying patrons showed up. That was at least better, though, than the attendance at some doubleheaders the previous year, when even matchups with the Yankees attracted crowds of fewer than 500.

But after winning their first nine games, the Browns seemingly lapsed into their old pattern, losing ten of their next fifteen games, and slipping into third place behind the Yankees and Senators. "Here in the east," said sportswriter Dan Daniel, "we still adhere to the notion that the American League race will settle down to another battle between the New York and Washington clubs." As for the Browns, he dismissed them as "the Luke Lollapaloozas."

In fact, though, the fearsome Yankees had plenty of wartime nobodies of their own. On July 2, shortstop Oscar Grimes made three errors in one inning, just short of the wartime record of four errors set by shortstop Lennie Merullo of the Cubs. Grimes was benched and replaced by Mike "Mollie" Milosevich, a twenty-nine-year-old rookie who in the off-season was a coal miner. Arthur Beauregard "Bud" Metheny, another twenty-nine-year-old, had knocked around the farm chain.

Halfway through the season, one of the St. Louis newspapers began running a symposium called "What's Wrong with the Browns?" Fans were showing little appreciation of the Browns' winning ways, and the newspaper wanted to know why attendance remained so low. Getting to the real bottom of the matter, it found all kinds of reasons why the fans were still staying home, even though the Browns were now setting a blistering pace: the hot dogs cost too much; the program had been hiked from five cents to ten cents; Sewell refused to call for sacrifice flies; he had traded away prized players like Johnny Niggeling, Rick Ferrell, and Harlond Clift, and got nothing in return; the beer cost too much; the park was hard to get to, in a bad neighborhood, and dirty; the Browns were simply not a colorful lot; and, finally, American League baseball was just not as much fun as the game played in the National League.

Yet the Browns "had guts, no losing streak beyond three games, and a most admirable quality of taking a ferocious beating in the first game of a doubleheader and coming back to win the second."

Sewell used pinch hitters and pinch runners, and fiddled with the starting lineup with remarkable frequency—and success—almost as though he were operating on a sixth sense. Midway through the season, Washington sportswriter Shirley Povich asked Sewell, "What's going on here,

Luke? You change these line-ups every day! You must smell these guys on the bench getting hot." Sewell replied, "No, Shirley, I smell those bums out there on the field getting cold." Talking about the success of his pitching staff and baseball strategy in general, Sewell once explained to another reporter, "I just tell 'em to throw it on in there. You can put me down as a man whose mind refuses to work more than 24 hours in advance. I don't know how many games anybody else is behind, and I don't care. I have enough to do right here."

Sewell was dealt a blow in midseason when Potter was thrown out of a game against the Yankees for using an illegal spitball and suspended from playing for ten days—the first pitcher to be suspended for throwing a spitball. During this period, Sewell relied on Galehouse, who had returned to full-time duty, while keeping an uneasy eye over his shoulder at the draft board.

The turning point for the Browns in the 1944 season was a double-header in Cleveland on July 16. Both games went to sixteen innings. In the first game, Gutteridge scored the deciding run, 8 to 7, on McQuinn's short pop fly to center with one out. In the second game, Gutteridge led off in the twelfth inning with a 350-foot triple and scored the winning run, 2 to 1, on Byrnes's fly. That put the Browns a full two games up on the Yankees. Sewell felt that in this doubleheader the team finally meshed and started to believe in itself. Why? "Those peculiar and mysterious crystallizations that sometimes hit ball clubs are almost inexplicable," he later recalled. "You are always looking for them, working toward them; and sometimes they come and sometimes they don't." On that July afternoon, the Browns crystallized, and they were to continue their winning ways through September.

Throughout the season, Jakucki not only threw hard but was a good hitter. Once he was pitching in a game against the Yankees in New York, and the Yankees were winning by one run in the eighth inning. Jakucki used an old-style bat without much of a knob. Walking up to Clary, who was sitting next to the bat rack, he said, "Where is that chickenshit bat you use?" Clary reached over, pulled it out, and handed it to him. Jakucki used it to hit a home run, which won the game for the Browns, but he never touched that kind of bat again.

After a game, Jakucki always showered quickly and was out of the locker room within ten minutes; others, like McQuinn, lingered and were the last ones out when the team was on the road because they had nowhere to go. Jakucki always headed for the bars. If it was a Monday,

McQuinn would say, "See you Thursday, Jack," and Jakucki would turn around, laugh, and take off. If it was a Thursday, McQuinn would say, "See you Monday, Jack." When he was not in the lineup, Jakucki simply disappeared for days on end.

Kreevich seldom drank much while in St. Louis because not only Sewell but his wife kept a close eye on him. On road trips, though, he was often drunk. "That's why damn near every night on the road—we were the same size, the same height, he was heavier than me—he would want to wrestle me," Clary later recalled. "If a man wants to wrestle you, you have to wrestle back or he'll kill ya. We wrestled in the Pullman cars up and down the aisles, rolling over and over. A carpet in a Pullman car is like sandpaper. It's rough, and I stayed skinned up."

Clary did his best to hide from Kreevich, but with no luck. When the team was traveling in a Pullman, Kreevich would walk down the aisles, parting the curtains and looking for Clary; when he found him, they wrestled. Kreevich also went hunting for his wrestling partner in hotels. Once, at the Shoreham Hotel in Washington, they started wrestling in a room and broke the bed. Clary dreaded his approach but never got mad. Later, after his retirement, he called Kreevich "the most underrated player I ever saw."

Kreevich was a powerful hitter, even though he had lost the index finger of his left hand. Once, batting against future Hall of Fame pitcher Hal Newhouser of the Detroit Tigers, he went 4 for 4. Returning to the bench after his last hit, he sat down next to Clary, held out his hand, displaying his three fingers and a thumb, and said, "I got me a whole handful."

On another occasion, the Browns were in Philadelphia, and Jakucki, Shirley, and some other players got drunk in the hotel bar and started causing a lot of mayhem. The men's room was up a flight of stairs on the mezzanine, and one of the players decided to urinate over the banister onto some hotel guests below. Jakucki and Shirley went after him, turning over tables and chairs and finally busting down the bathroom door to get hold of the miscreant. "But something like that was common with them guys," Clary recalled.

Another day in Philadelphia, Vernon Stephens went to Shibe Park, sat down next to Clary, and said, "I don't think I can make it today. I haven't slept a wink all night." He had been out with some woman. Russ Christopher, a tall sidearmer, was pitching for the Athletics, and he struck Stephens out three times. But in the ninth inning, Stephens went up to bat again. This time the ball hit the roof of the upper deck and won the game for the Browns. "Stephens could hit the ball," Mark Christman later recalled. "He could swing. He hit 25 home runs in that big ball park at Sportsman's Park, a long way for a right-handed hitter."

As the pennant race tightened, Bill DeWitt called Stephens into his office. DeWitt told him, "Vern, for criminy's sakes, we've got a chance to win this pennant. Now why don't you take care of yourself and quit running around at night, and get in bed and get your rest? Because you can help us, you're the best hitter on the ball club. With your help we can win this thing and make some money out of it."

"All right," Stephens agreed.

For the next three weeks, he gave up drinking and going out at night and never got a base hit. Frustrated, DeWitt called him back into his office and said, "Go out and stay out!"

Jack Kramer called his mother in New Orleans every night, whether he was in his room at the Melbourne Hotel in St. Louis or on the road. He had been married to Dotty Dotson, a well-known singer in Del Courtney's band, but they were separated. He liked to dress up and sometimes changed clothes two or three times a day, which led some of his teammates to deride him as a "fruit basket." But Clary told them, "You'll find out if you mess with him." Clary also reminded them that Dotty Dotson was a beautiful woman.

By August the buzz in New York was all about the Browns, with Associated Press sportswriter Chip Royal noting, "In the neighborhood drug store, the barber shop on the side street, or the joint around the corner, there's only one topic of conversation among baseball fans: the St. Louis Browns. As one wag put it, instead of singing the 'St. Louis Blues,' they're wailing about the St. Louis Browns. The stool managers can't figure out how a team without an outstanding star, picked by the experts to finish in the second division, can beat all the other American League contenders in the flag chase."

As the Browns struggled to capture the American League flag and make the Streetcar Series a reality, the city's streetcars figured in another drama that hot and humid August. Thousands of laborers, many from the Deep South and many of them black, had migrated to St. Louis to fill jobs created by the war effort. They found ready employment because the government awarded defense contracts only to industries that abided by guidelines set down in 1941 by the Fair Employment Practices Committee that sought to abolish racial and sex discrimination in the workplace.

Though blacks and whites now found themselves working side by side during the day, racial prejudice was not so easily abolished. A few scuffles broke out on the streetcars between white passengers and black women on their way to work. On the morning of August 6, a white man died of a brain hemorrhage after being punched by a black youth. The two men had argued after the white man insisted on smoking on the streetcar.

Racial tensions threatened to erupt, just as they had in Detroit the year before when more than thirty persons were killed and hundreds injured during a race riot. In an editorial, the *Post-Dispatch* "called for both races to come to their senses, and said that the idea of racial superiority was typical of Nazi minds." Eventually, racial tensions ebbed, and calm was restored.

By August summer had become a blast furnace, baking the ballpark until a crust of hard dirt formed on the infield, giving the Browns one more obstacle to overcome. "The groundskeepers never really got a chance to work on the field because either the Browns or the Cardinals were playing a game every day," recalled Gutteridge. "By August, there really wasn't any grass left at all. To play infield on that, you really had to play. You had to be a good infielder."

The Browns slumped in August, playing twenty-two straight games on the road—winning just nine of the contests. Sewell, ever the thinker, understood why his team began losing precisely at that moment. First of all, the Browns were largely made up of veteran players, none of whom had ever played on a pennant winner before. Some of them were no doubt suffering from what the manager called "pennantitis," the pressure or mental strain of the pennant race. Pennantitis almost always struck a team in contention in September, and pennantitis was responsible for a good many pennant races being blown.

As late as September 7, the Tigers still saw the Yankees, not the Browns, as the team to beat. Four teams were making the American League pennant race the tightest since 1908, when Detroit, Cleveland, Chicago, and St. Louis fought it out until the last few days of the season, and Detroit had won on the final day.

It was in September, in Cleveland, that Sewell read the letter from his friend Ty Cobb to the Browns, telling them that they could win, and that the greatest ballplayer in history believed in them. The important thing, as always with Sewell, was *believing*. He was not trying to sell his players a gimmick or salesman's ploy. He believed in his heart that his team could win the pennant, and he made sure that the players believed in their hearts that they could, too.

At long last, the Browns returned home to Sportsman's Park. Unfortunately, during a four-game series with Detroit, their last with the Tigers for the year, they lost another three out of four. That gave the Browns thirteen defeats in eighteen games. Cobb's vote of confidence appeared to be having no effect.

The outlook for the last four games of the season—all against the Yankees—was not brilliant: Detroit was playing Washington, which never won, and the Browns had to match the Tigers win for win. On Thursday, the first game was called because of rain. The next day was a doubleheader, but only 6,172 fans showed up, because everyone assumed the odds that the Browns could win the pennant were hopeless. But Kramer won the first game, 4 to 1, and then Potter shut out the Yankees in the second, 1 to 0. Then, on Saturday, Galehouse won 2 to 0 after Kreevich saved the game with a spectacular catch. Johnny Lindell hit a line drive that broke like a curveball. Kreevich was running after it in dead center field, looking over his right shoulder, when the ball broke back. In desperation, he stuck his glove behind his head and somehow managed to catch the ball without looking at it.

Then came an even more spine-tingling, nail-biting thriller against the Yankees on October 1, when Laabs hit his two historic home runs. Those homers, in Sewell's mind, were the culmination of a long chain of events that went all the way back to 1926 when he became a regular ballplayer instead of being shunted off to the minors. It went back to Tris Speaker's giving him a chance to play, and to Alva Bradley's begging him to talk to Don Barnes.

"We didn't win the pennant on Laabs' homer," Sewell later recalled. "We won it on a million other pitches clear back to 1926 and beyond—every pitch in itself *meaning* something, that helped win the first American League pennant for St. Louis in 1944."

In the clubhouse after the last game, amid the hilarity and the screaming, the handshaking, yelling, singing, laughter, confusion, and excitement, the realization of the Browns' heroic accomplishment slowly began to dawn on Sewell. Nothing like this had ever happened to him. He felt completely limp, and shuddered when he thought how close it all was—how a thousand times a single ball could have beaten the team.

Yet the big moment was still to come. That occurred when he finally left the clubhouse and headed for the Chase Hotel, where the Browns were hosting a party for the team. As Sewell walked in, he heard his wife—who always sat in the first seat just to the right of the Browns' dugout—screaming hysterically, "We won! We won! We won!"

Then all the emotion built up over a lifetime came rushing up.

"It was great, wasn't it?" he said to his wife. "Why don't you just let it go?"

Then she just broke down and cried, and the knees of the man who was baseball's man of the hour buckled too. For the first time since winning the American League pennant earlier that day, Luke Sewell cried as he hugged his wife.

Bill DeWitt never would tell Sewell who had recommended him for the Browns job, but the manager later acknowledged that his anonymous benefactor "had made a Cinderella out of me."

The Half-Apple Curve

Bob Broeg was a twenty-five-year-old marine who had a problem—in fact, two or three problems, and one was worse than the other. In June 1943, only fifteen months earlier, he had gotten married. His first year of marriage with Dorth had been idyllic, until Broeg received notification, without any advance warning, that he had been transferred from St. Louis to marine headquarters in suburban Washington. Leaving Dorth had been tough. Now he was lovesick and homesick, missing not only his young bride but also his mom's lemon meringue pie. To make matters worse, the Cardinals had once again wrapped up the National League pennant, meaning that some games of the World Series would once again be played in his hometown. Wonder of wonders, there was even the possibility of a first ever Streetcar Series if the Browns, that other St. Louis team, did the impossible and won the American League pennant.

Broeg's love for the Cardinals had begun when he was twelve years old and took a streetcar to see Frankie Frisch and his Gashouse Gang for $1 a ticket. Broeg's parents subscribed to all four local papers so he could devour every detail of each Redbirds game. After attending a local South Side high school, he graduated from the University of Missouri in Columbia with a journalism degree and went to work for the Associated Press bureau in Boston in 1941. Later, before he was drafted, he got a job covering sports for the *St. Louis Star-Times*.

Dorth, like her husband an apprentice sportswriter in civilian life, loved baseball. The previous year, when they were still courting, he had taken her to the Browns' home opener against the Chicago White Sox. He quickly noticed, as he later wrote, something about the ball: "The Spalding Company had manufactured an ersatz ball, called the 'balata,' a poor green-tree substitute for precious war-time rubber." The balata ball was "mushy," and as a result home runs became scarce. Even Dorth noticed that there was something wrong with the ball. "We were always kidding about it," Cardinals star shortstop Marty Marion later recalled. "But nobody really questioned it. If that's what we were going to play with, that's what we were going to play with."

On another day, watching the Cardinals sweep a doubleheader over the Dodgers, Broeg and his fiancée saw Brooklyn right-hander Les Webber irritate slugger Stan Musial, who was then en route to his first batting championship. Webber decked Musial with his first pitch, then forced him to back away from three high-and-tight deliveries. For the first and only time in his career, an enraged Musial headed out to the mound, only to be restrained by catcher Mickey Owen and plate umpire Al Barlick.

In Washington, Broeg had followed the Cardinals from afar and also caught a few Senators home games. During the Browns' momentous struggle against the Yankees in the last four games of the regular season, he was sitting at his desk, listening to the Senators-Tigers game. "They were feeding in results," he later recalled. "My brother-in-law had come in with a rare bottle of scotch from Canada and we were nibbling on that and, of course, I was pulling for the Browns."

Just then, his boss, a major, came into the office. Marine "researchers," the major told the disbelieving young soldier, had discovered that four members of the Baseball Writers' Association of America were in the corps. Three of them were in the Pacific, presumably all combat correspondents. So the marines' entertainment monthly, *Leatherneck*, wanted Broeg to cover all the Series games for their special Pacific editions, wherever the games might be held, at their expense!

That was the first miracle. Broeg could only hope against hope for a second—a pennant win by the Browns. After Sewell's swashbucklers won three straight from the third-place Yankees, he could hardly contain himself, but when he heard that Sig Jakucki was going to pitch for the Browns on the final-day showdown, his heart sank. Jakucki, he remembered, was "the grizzled guy who had angrily draped a semi-pro ump off the bridge at Wichita's Arkansas River." But after "Bill DeWitt's carefully contrived roster of castoffs and cutthroats, 4-Fs, and players able to escape from war plants" won the pennant, as Broeg later wrote, his impossible dream came true. St. Louis was going to play host to an all-Midwest World Series.

As a marine, Broeg also knew that this World Series was not just a game. For a few precious moments, as he later recalled, it would help people forget there was a war on. "It was as if time stood still for a week."

The daily deprivations everyone had to put up with could temporarily be forgotten, though no doubt the hearts of some would ache that a "father didn't live to see the Browns win or that a brother, son, nephew, and dear friend was tied down in a European hedgerow or Pacific foxhole."

Broeg told his hometown folks that if they did not mind, he would have to spend most of his time downtown at a hotel. For press parties, Browns owner Don Barnes was somehow able to put on a lavish display of whiskey, beer, gin, and champagne. Broeg did not want to miss out on any of the celebrations—the lemon meringue pie would have to wait.

Another sportswriter, Jack Hand of the Associated Press, who at the start of the season had picked the Browns to finish at the bottom of the standings, was still dismissive of the American League team. His reasons were unassailable. "With a standout outfield built around Stan Musial, an infield hinged on 'Mr. Shortstop,' a catching department that includes Walker Cooper, and a strong arm mound staff of Mort Cooper, Ted Wilks, and Harry Brecheen, the Redbirds stick out in all departments with the possible exception of pitching."

The Browns' stellar pitching staff was only one reason to give some sportswriters second thoughts, the Cardinals management ulcers, and Browns fans hope. Another possible reason was a fear that perhaps the Cardinals had gotten so complacent that they could not possibly fight their way out of their end-of-season slump. If the Browns had scratched and clawed their way to the top berth on the very last day of the season, the Redbirds had spent the entire month of September coasting—mostly downhill. That month, they had won only five games, while losing fifteen.

On the other hand, a cynic might have pointed out, perhaps the Cardinals were simply bored with winning. Even with that September record, they had still run away with the National League pennant, finishing 14 ½ games ahead of Pittsburgh, their nearest competitor. During one week in the regular season, they stood 73-27, and eventually finished with a 105-49 record, for a .682 winning percentage. They had won their 90th game (or more than the Browns won in the entire season) on August 28, earlier than any other team since the Chicago Cubs accomplished that same feat in 1906. Not even the Cardinals, though, or any other team, has ever been able to equal or better the Cubs' winning percentage of 76.3 percent of its games—a record that still stands.

Among the fans who had no doubt that the Browns could do the impossible was a contingent from Cape Girardeau, where the Browns had been training for the past two years. "It took Cape Girardeau just two years to do what Florida and California couldn't do in 40 years," Mayor Raymond E. Beckman proudly boasted. The *Southeast Missourian* quoted local fans as saying, "They'll take those Cardinals like Patton took France!" Unfortunately, wartime restrictions on travel made it impossible for most out-of-town rooters for either the Browns or the Cardinals to get to St. Louis to see the Series, even if they could get tickets. Both teams had to adhere to Office of Defense Transportation restrictions and sell virtually all their tickets in the immediate metropolitan area of St. Louis.

One observer who wondered whether the Cardinals just might be in trouble was John Drebinger of the *New York Times*. As "the game's outstanding academic minds" pondered the relative merits of the two teams, he noted that if the Series had been played even a month earlier, the outcome would never have been in doubt. The Cardinals, "rocketing to their third straight flag," would have been the unanimous, unqualified choice to win, no matter who their opponent was. Until August, he went on to say, "the Redbirds were so thoroughly the class of anything either league had to offer that a comparison would have been ridiculous." Nor had the military draft depleted their roster as it had that of virtually every other team. One exception was second baseman Lou Klein, but the Cardinals had come up with Billy Verban as his replacement, and as it turned out he was just as good as Klein.

The Redbirds were flying high, Drebinger ominously reported, until "suddenly, almost overnight, something passed out of [manager] Billy Southworth's array of 'invincibles.' They began to lose." Even though their overwhelming lead kept them out of danger of losing the pennant, they were nevertheless beginning to play an awful lot like "vulnerables." Perhaps that was true, but as *The Sports Encyclopedia* later noted, the 1944 Cardinals team won its third pennant in a row "in the most one-sided race in the [National League] in 40 years."

If the Browns' winning the American League pennant had been improbable enough, for them now to go ahead and take the Series against the Cardinals seemed simply inconceivable. After all, the Cardinals did not appear to have any weaknesses, whether in hitting, pitching, or defense. The team boasted a composite .275 batting average, 100 home runs, and a .402 slugging percentage—all three the best in the major leagues. Its pitchers had tossed twenty-six shutouts, or nine more than the next National League team, while the pitching staff's 2.67 ERA was well below the 3.09 that the Detroit Tigers recorded to lead the American League.

Only once before had a team racked up three straight hundred-win seasons, and that was back when the venerable Connie Mack accomplished that feat with the Philadelphia Athletics in 1929–31.

More statistics only added to the mystique of the Cardinals as a team that was all but invincible. For example, not only was their .982 fielding percentage the best in either league, but their 112 errors committed broke the all-time record for fewest errors by one team in a season.

The Browns did have a few statistics on their side, especially—or rather, almost exclusively—regarding their pitching. In the last nine games of the regular season, the team had allowed only 10 runs and finished with a 3.17 ERA and 16 shutouts (second only to Detroit), and led the league in strikeouts. The Browns' fielding was a respectable .972, and both Christman and McQuinn led the league in fielding at their respective positions.

Other statistics were not so favorable. The team's collective batting average of .252 was the second worst in the league. No other team had ever made it to the World Series with such a low percentage except for the Red Sox, who in 1918 squeaked by with a .249 average. The Browns also would have become the first team in history to win the pennant without a single .300 hitter or a twenty-game winner on the squad if Kreevich had not collected two hits on the final day of the season to bring his average up to .301.

The Cardinals' 1944 lineup was virtually the same as the 1943 team that had fallen to the Yankees in the World Series. The two most notable changes were Johnny Hopp, a backup outfielder and first baseman in 1943, who now took over in center field for Harry "The Hat" Walker, and Emil Verban at second base. Verban, the Redbirds' third second baseman in three years, was generally regarded as the team's weakest link, with a batting average of only .257.

Ray Sanders, at first base for the Cardinals, had batted .295 with 12 homers and 102 RBIs, for a tie for fourth place in the league. His .994 fielding percentage also led the National League at first base, and equaled that of McQuinn for the Browns. At shortstop was the stellar Marion, the league's MVP for 1944. Affectionately known as "Slats" or "The Octopus," the six-foot-two Marion had hit a modest .267 with only 6 homers and 63 RBIs during the season. But his .972 fielding percentage led the league at shortstop.

Rounding out the infield were steady-as-she-goes Whitey Kurowski at third base and catcher Walker Cooper. In the regular season Cooper had hit .317 with 13 homers and 72 RBIs, while Kurowski turned in a respectable .270 percentage with 20 homers. Hopp had posted some fantastic numbers for his first year as a starter—a league-leading fielding percentage of .997 at third base, and a .336 batting average that placed him fourth in the standings. He also hit 11 home runs, scored 106 runs, drove in 72, and stole a team-high 15 bases. Marty Marion later explained the relatively low base-stealing number this way: "Back in our day we didn't do much running. We had a pretty fast team but our manager believed in first and third and all that kind of stuff. We didn't do much stealing."

Danny Litwhiler, a power hitter picked up in 1943 to replace the irreplaceable Enos "Country" Slaughter, who had entered military service before the opening of the season, now owned left field. Though he hit only .264 with 15 homers, his RBI average was a respectable 82.

Right field, of course, belonged to one of the greatest players in the game, Stan Musial. Only twenty-three years old, Musial was eligible to be drafted, but because his hometown of Donora, Pennsylvania, had more than enough eligible draftees already, he had yet to be called—much to the relief and delight of the fans. In 1943 Musial had won the MVP award, and this season had hit .347, the second highest in the league. He also led the league with 197 hits, 51 doubles, and a .549 slugging percentage. His 14 triples tied for fourth in the National League, and he had also chalked up 12 homers, 112 runs (second in the league), and 94 RBIs while drawing 90 walks (third best in the league) and striking out only 28 times.

The Cardinals' pitching staff was virtually intact from its pennant-winning 1943 season; only one new pitcher had a chance of starting a game in the Series—rookie Ted Wilks. Mort Cooper, Walker's older brother, who led the rotation, had won the 1942 MVP award when he went 27-7 with 10 shutouts and a 1.78 ERA. The 1944 season marked the third straight time he had compiled a twenty-win season, finishing with a 22-7 record, a 2.46 ERA, and a league-high seven shutouts. In short, three Cardinals players had been named MVP for three years in a row.

The other pitchers on the starting staff were Max Lanier (17-12, 2.65), Harry Brecheen (16-5, 2.85), reliever Blix Donnelly (2-1, 2.12), Freddy Schmidt (7-3, 3.15), and Al Jurisch (7-9, 3.39), who split his time between starting and relief.

"Goddamn," the Browns' Ellis Clary was later to recall, reflecting on a Cardinals roster that boasted Musial, Kurowski, both Coopers, and Marion, "they had a hell of a team."

Unlike the previous two World Series, the first six games of the Browns-Cardinals matchup were to be played on six consecutive days, because the two teams played in the same park. The only off day, if one became necessary, was scheduled to take place before the seventh game. From a strategic point of view, that meant the pitcher who started in game 1 would most likely not pitch three games, unless he pitched on only two days' rest for the deciding seventh game. That left Sewell with a serious decision to make about who would start on Wednesday, October 4, the first day of the Series.

Most sportswriters and baseball connoisseurs thought Nelson Potter was the obvious choice to get the nod. Despite his ten-game suspension earlier in the year for throwing an illegal spitball, he led the Browns with 19 wins and also had a 2.83 ERA. In the stretch he had performed admirably, going 6-1 in September. Both of his final two starts were shutouts. One sportswriter who begged to differ was New York–based Dan Daniel, who in a story filed October 3 opined that Jack Kramer was the probable choice to face Mort Cooper in game 1. Like Potter, Kramer had piled up an enviable record during the Browns' stunning September drive, finishing all six games that he started and winning five of them. In that month, he had also pitched a total of 58 ⅔ innings, allowing only 8 runs on 39 hits, and 5 walks, while striking out 26. Though his season record stood at 17–13, his 2.49 ERA was the lowest among the Browns starters.

The choice, then, was a toss-up. Both Kramer and Potter had pitched one game each in the Browns' doubleheader sweep over the Yankees on September 28, and now both were rested. Thus the announcement Sewell made on October 3, the day before the opening of the Series, came as a complete shock to just about everyone—except to Denny Galehouse, who had been sworn to secrecy when the manager told him he was going to start. Sewell's surprise choice had finished the season with a 9-10 record, and for September was just 3-4, but he had allowed only two runs in his last three regular starts, and Sewell had a hunch.

Galehouse had not even been with the team at spring training. A man who had started his major-league career in Cleveland back in 1934, he had failed to distinguish himself in one mediocre season after another before being traded to the Boston Red Sox in December 1938. He proved to be no better in Bean Town, and two years later, when the Browns came shopping, Boston sent him to St. Louis. According to one account, the desperate Browns paid $30,000 for Galehouse and pitcher Fritz Ostermueller, but the purchase was hardly much of a bargain. Galehouse's pitching did get a little better, and in 1941 his record was 9-10, with a career-best 3.64 ERA. In 1942 he finished with a 12-12 record and a 3.62 ERA, and then topped that with an 11-11 record and a 2.77 ERA in 1943. That same year, he threw two shutouts and held opponents to two or fewer runs eleven times. But when spring-training time came around in 1944, Galehouse sent word that he was going to continue working at his Goodyear aircraft job in Akron and retire from baseball. In his spare time he coached a high school baseball team in nearby Cuyahoga Falls, and that was enough to keep his hand in the game.

That seemed to be that until pitcher Steve Sundra was drafted and the Browns, finding themselves in an even more desperate pickle than usual, persuaded Galehouse to reconsider. Galehouse did his own spring training, playing catch with friends in the neighborhood and running around on local streets to get into condition. Despite his best efforts, as he later admitted, he was not nearly in as good physical shape as his teammates when, on May 14 in Philadelphia, he made his first appearance. On that day, he did well enough, pitching one and a third innings in scoreless relief. But thereafter his troubles began. He lost two games in May, including one start, and the following month started three times but lost twice. During that latter period he had given up 11 runs on 17 hits while striking out just 3.

But Galehouse had spirit and determination and was not a quitter. Let go by the team, he went back home and signed up with the Akron Orphans of the Akron–Barberton–Cuyahoga Falls League, pitching for them in a kind of catch-up spring/summer training program. On June 21, when he led his team to an 8 to 2 victory over the Barberton Genets, the Genets groused about having to face a major-league pitcher and lodged an official complaint to the league office shortly after the contest. Two weeks later, league officials ruled that Galehouse was an ineligible player.

In mid-July Galehouse finally rejoined the Browns as a full-time player after receiving an assurance from his draft board that he would not be inducted into the army until after the season ended. Though he still never recaptured his peak pitching form, he did win three games that month, and ended the season with a 3.12 ERA. Clearly, his record was spotty at best, and no doubt everyone had to wonder just what Sewell was thinking when he nominated this part-time, home-conditioned, lackluster pitcher as the man who would face the formidable Cardinals in game 1. Maybe it was because Sewell knew that Galehouse had something to prove, once and for all, to himself—and to the fans, the sportswriters, and his teammates.

On the second-to-last day of the season, after Galehouse had shut out the Yankees while allowing just five singles, Sewell approached him in private in the locker room. Galehouse was just the opposite of Jakucki, who made a point of being out of the ballpark as quickly as possible. The big Ohio pitcher was a heavy sweater, and he preferred to take his time showering. When he finally emerged, his teammates were usually gone or getting dressed. Sewell came over to Galehouse while he was alone, and told the pitcher that if the Browns won the pennant, he was going to start.

"If we're in it, you're it," Sewell said.

"Okay, fine," Galehouse merely replied.

He knew that everyone on the team was speculating who would be the starter, but Sewell told him to keep mum about it. "We were told to keep quiet, yeah," Galehouse later recalled. "She [his wife] knew enough to keep quiet."

Sewell even kept up the suspense after the Browns won the pennant, and waited for two days, until after the Browns had completed a two-and-a-half-hour workout on October 3, before making the announcement that Potter, who had won nineteen games, would not be the starter. Instead, as any baseball statistician knew, a man who had the worst season winning percentage of any pitcher ever to start a World Series opener was going to be given that honor. The baseball world was stunned.

GALEHOUSE SURPRISE CHOICE TO PITCH FOR BROWNS, an understated *Post-Dispatch* headline reported the next day. Another local paper, the *Star-Times*, was not so timid, calling the selection of Galehouse "the first bombshell of the 1944 World Series." Pressed on who might pitch in games 2, 3, or 4, Sewell wisecracked, "It might rain all winter, and we may not get to use anyone."

Young Broeg reported the surprise to his fellow marines in the Pacific this way: "In the language of the baseball dugout, where the polysyllable is of unknown quantity, Luke Sewell had 'more guts than a burglar' by taking a gamble unequalled in 15 years in the choice of an opening-day selection for a World Series. But a tall, thin man with a high collar and watery blue eyes, sitting less than 100 feet away from the Browns' bench, could have told him that the risk isn't always as great as it seems."

Broeg was referring to the legendary Connie Mack. Before the opening game of the 1929 World Series between his Philadelphia Athletics and

Hundreds of fans waited in the cold to try to score bleacher seats for game 1 of the 1944 World Series. (Arteaga Photos)

the Chicago Cubs, Mack had confounded the experts by passing up his pitching aces, Lefty Grove and George Earnshaw, to start a graying veteran who for months, as Broeg quipped, "had sat around just listening to his arteries harden." But mentally and physically the Chicago sluggers had trained for the blistering fastball of Earnshaw and Grove. Mack had a hunch that Howard Ehmke's slow curve and half-speed ball would throw the Cubs off stride. He gambled—and won, with Ehmke giving up only 3 hits and striking out 13 batters for a Series record that still stood, and beating the puzzled Chicagoans, 3 games to 1.

Sewell also announced that catcher Red Hayworth and outfielders Chet Laabs and Mike Kreevich would play in every game, no matter what.

For game 1, on October 4, a few dark clouds appeared in the sky just after sunrise, and by 8:15 a light rain had begun to fall.

Concessionaires were prepared for a capacity crowd, having loaded up with 40,000 frankfurters, a truckload of peanuts, 10,000 cases of soda, and 5,000 cases of beer. Blake Harper, the man in charge of concessions, maintained strict neutrality by making sure that an equal number of Browns and Cardinals pennants were on sale to the public.

Assigned to seat the crowd were 250 ushers, who arrived at 7:30 a.m. and began lining up chairs in their proper places and drilling for the big job ahead. At 9:50, workmen swarmed onto the field and began removing the tarpaulins to give the damp earth underneath an opportunity to dry out. One groundskeeper spent more than an hour currying the pitcher's mound. At 10:00 a twenty-piece band took the field and began tuning up for the great day ahead.

The long line of fans waiting to purchase tickets were all in a partying, festive mood. Some played cards or craps, while others danced to jitter-bug music provided by students from nearby Soldan High School. A few enterprising neighborhood children took advantage of the situation by selling cartons or boxes as makeshift seats. The *Post-Dispatch* reported that "a Negro boy rented 19 of 25 collapsible chairs for 50 cents."

One baseball eminence who would not be attending the Series was none other than Judge Kenesaw Mountain Landis, the first baseball commissioner, who was suffering from a bad cold. A former U.S. district court judge from Illinois, Landis had come into power in 1920 in the wake of the Chicago Black Sox gambling scandal of 1919, taking the place of a three-man commission that had overseen baseball since 1903. Back in 1907, Landis had earned a national reputation as an incorruptible magistrate who imposed a $29 million fine on Standard Oil for accepting illegal rail-freight rebates. The decision was later reversed, but Landis's integrity and character were never questioned.

Despite missing the Series for the first time since he was hired, Landis still made sure that the Series was not called by radio broadcaster and ex-Cardinals pitcher Dizzy Dean. Much as the colorful Dean contributed to enthusiasm for the game, Landis arranged for a more professional announcer to sit in the upstairs booth.

The Series was being covered by reporters from twenty-one states, as well as by three Canadian papers and one in Panama, along with three G.I. papers, seven movie studios, and several national weekly magazines, including *Newsweek*, *Life*, and *Look*. The Mutual Radio Network was broadcasting the games on a nationwide hookup, numerous local and out-of-town broadcasters were set to give live play-by-play descriptions or summaries of the contests, and American troops abroad were able to hear the games live via broadcasts over short-wave radio. The novice sportswriter assigned to cover the Series for Panama was a seventeen-year-old boy named Rafael Aleman, while the oldest veteran in the broadcast booth was Joe Page, eighty-four years old, a reporter for the *Montreal Star*, who had covered every Series since 1884, back when the Browns played Providence RI.

Among the big-name sportswriters in attendance was Grantland Rice, the man who had memorably described the Notre Dame backfield as the "Four Horsemen of the Apocalypse." He was there on assignment from the North American Newspaper Alliance. Others included Orlo Robertson and Charles Dunkley of the Associated Press, Bob Considine of International News Service, Sgt. Charles Kiles of *Stars and Stripes*, and Bob Broeg, the St. Louis native now with the marines, who had lucked into the assignment for *Leatherneck*, the official publication of the Marine Corps.

In all, about 250 reporters were keeping seventy Western Union telegraph operators busy on direct wires to their newspapers during and after each game. In addition, another twenty-five telegraph operators were stationed at the park to take stories directly after the game. In the mornings and evenings, twenty to thirty operators were stationed at the Hotel Jefferson in downtown St. Louis, where many of the journalists were staying, to transmit stories from a pressroom early each morning and late each night. On the day before game 1, reporters filed 130,000 words, while on the first day of the Series the word count reached 175,000. Millions more words were being transmitted by radio. At war plants, factories, and other workplaces, many employees were allowed to listen to the games, or at least updates, while they worked. At one plant, a buzzer would sound, riveting would immediately halt, and over the loudspeaker would come a quick update about a recent score.

The American League was also making movies with sound of all the games. Immediately after the Series ended, 320 prints were to be developed and sent for distribution overseas to the armed services, with an expected delivery date of about November 1. Another 200 prints were to be made for showings to civilians in the United States, though those prints were not expected to be available until January 1, 1945.

Several newsreel outfits had also taken up position on the roof of the grandstand to photograph highlights of the games. Among those represented were Paramount, Movietone, Pathé, News of the Day, and Universal Newsreel. Not to be outdone, the Missouri State Highway Department was also taking color film of the Series for use in advertising the state.

The Browns' World Series ticket, something never before seen in base-ball, was identical to that of the Cardinals, except that it was printed with a brown background instead of cardinal red. The Browns' game tickets were for games 3, 4, and 5. Proceeds of games 3, 4, and 6 were to go to the National War Relief fund.

The earliest "early bird" waiting to buy a ticket was Cardinals fan Arthur "Happy" Felsh, who had taken up residence in an oblong, canvas-covered cardboard shack outside the pavilion gate a week before. Felsh had been the first to wait outside the gate for the past sixteen years, but in 1943 he had moved out of St. Louis and so been obliged to store his movable residence at a local YMCA after the Cardinals lost the previous year's Series. This year he furnished it with a cot, mattress, blankets, and even an electric light and promised that next year he would try to install a shower.

Another fan who lined up outside the park in the predawn hours was a die-hard Browns booster named Sisler Brown Futrell, a twenty-two-year-old sailor who had been named not only for the team but for the great Browns first baseman. Sisler told reporters he had spent three and a half years in the South Pacific and that the submarine he was aboard had sunk twenty-seven Japanese vessels. Other fans braved a chilling wind and temperatures in the low sixties, sleeping on boxes, chairs, and the sidewalk to be among the first in line to buy tickets to the bleachers and pavilions. By 3 a.m. their number reached only 300, but two hours later another 1,000 showed up.

"This rain don't bother me," sixteen-year-old Bill Schneider told a reporter. "A loyal baseball fan would sit through a snowstorm."

In the stands was the Browns' oldest fan, retired druggist Charles H. Zahn, ninety-three years old, who had been rooting for the team since 1869, four years after the Civil War ended. Pfc. Bill Veeck, general manager of the champion Milwaukee Brewers, was another spectator. Now a marine stationed in the Pacific, he had obtained leave to attend the Series. After the war, in 1951, he was to become the next—and last—owner of the Browns and to go on to make baseball history in a way no one ever had before, or ever has since. Sitting just a few rows away was nattily dressed Leo Durocher, manager of the Brooklyn Dodgers, the Browns' mirror image in the National League.

Enos Slaughter, the Cardinals' slugging outfielder, had also managed to get a furlough for the Series. Earlier he had stopped by the ballpark to work out with his old teammates. Currently, he was stationed at the army base in San Antonio, and during the season had led the San Antonio military league with a batting average of .419.

A few quarrels and shoving matches occasionally broke out in the bleachers among fans, most having to do with the relative merits of the two teams about to take the field, but on the whole, according to the *St. Louis Star-Times*, "the decorum of the crowd was excellent."

One man not pleased at all by the crowd was Walter Ridley, who earned his living selling peanuts to the fans at Sportsman's Park. Ridley had come to the notice of both baseball connoisseurs and a reporter for the *Sporting News* for his skill "at tossing the bags to the customers seated out of range." He was equally skillful at snatching the coin flung to him in payment. "Some of Walter's catches of flying coins in mid-air have been quite spectacular and have drawn favorable comment from the fans. And sometimes, particularly when Brooklyn is in town, odious comparisons are made between Ridley's defenses at retaining thrown objects and that of the athletes on the field. Walter rarely loses a nickel."

What bothered Ridley during the Series, surprisingly, was all the people. "With a big crowd you can't get through to make your sales," he explained. "When you can't get through a crowd you can only sell in a limited area. And any salesman can tell you that when you work a limited area you reach the saturation point that much sooner and are thus faced with a consumer shortage and a goods surplus." An artist, a businessman, and a philosopher, Ridley packaged each of the bags of peanuts he sold by hand.

Among the many sideshows at the World Series that Broeg described for his readers in the Pacific was "an aged Ohio screwball" named Harry Thobe, who showed up at the stadium dressed like a lunatic carnival barker with one red shoe and one white, a white suit, a red tonguelike tie, a flat-brimmed straw hat the color of the rainbow, a cane, and a parasol. A well-known gate-crasher (by invitation), he was a perennial presence at every World Series and Rose Bowl game, taking vacations from his regular job as a bricklayer. Once upon a time, he claimed, his teeth were filled with fourteen diamond fillings, but when the Depression came along he had to hock the eleven that were now missing.

Also sitting in the stands were Sewell's brother Joe, and Southworth's son, Major Billy Southworth Jr., who in December 1940 had become the first professional baseball player to sign up for the military.

A tongue-in-cheek item in the *Star-Times*, datelined "Astride a Fence" in Sportsman's Park, reported on the predicament of Bobby Scanlon, who during the regular season served as batboy for both the Cardinals and the Browns. Who was he rooting for? a reporter named Stan Mockler wondered. "Step right up and pick a winner, Bobby." The "slim, nervous, black-haired 18-year-old" took a deep breath and shouted, "And lose my job—two jobs?"

As Scanlon headed into the Cardinals' clubhouse, pursued by Mockler, Blix Donnelly joined in the fun, saying, with a wink to the reporter, "I think you're for the Browns, Bobby. I saw you shining up to Denny Galehouse."

"Oh, no, I'm not," the boy sputtered. "You see, I—"

"That's fine, then," Donnelly replied, cutting him off. "Glad to know you are backing the Cardinals. We think it's good luck to have a batboy in our dugout."

"No, you don't, Blix," Scanlon plaintively replied. "That ain't playing fair. You mugs are putting me behind the eight ball. I gotta stay neutral."

Just then, somebody in the Browns' dressing room upstairs called for Scanlon, and with a weary sigh he took off. When he got there, second baseman Don Gutteridge greeted him with a question: "Got any bets on the Series?"

"I don't bet," said Scanlon.

"You mean to say," said Gutteridge, "that you're not willing to risk a bob on us after we went and voted you in on the Series melon? That's gratitude for—"

"Well," said Scanlon, "you see, I got inside dope the Cardinals are going to do that, too, and—"

"Oh, he's a money player," Vern Stephens chipped in. "And what were you doing in there shining Mort Cooper's shoes? Trying to play both ends against the middle, eh?"

Facing the most miserable and yet happiest days of his life, Scanlon threw up his arms in disgust and muttered, "If only there was some way this damn thing could end in a tie!"

Another devoted fan of baseball watching the Series was Dr. Alexander Paul, a longtime teacher and missionary for the Disciples of Christ Church in Japan and China, who had spent more than twenty years in Asia after sailing from Vancouver for the Far East in 1922, accompanied by a group of major leaguers who were touring and playing in Asia. The missionary had only recently returned to the United States after being interned for most of the war by Japanese forces. On the morning of December 8, 1941, Dr. Paul, then in Nanking, had been visited by a detachment of Japanese soldiers, who searched his home. Several of the soldiers who could speak English were especially interested in the American's pile of the *Sporting News*, representing more than a year's worth of issues.

"Baseball!" one of the soldiers shouted, and an argument quickly ensued over how the papers would be distributed. Dr. Paul was later held in solitary confinement in his schoolroom. To pass the time, he once decided to pick his all-time All-Star team. He managed to send his choices by Chinese servants to another missionary being held in another part of the building, who then sent back his own selections.

Back in September, when the White Sox played the Browns at Sportsman's Park during the home stretch, one reporter noted that the infield, badly torn up after being used nearly every day of the season, "resembled a wheat field that had been badly shorn by a mowing machine." In fact, in the fifth inning of that game, Chicago player Hal Trosky raised his hand to call time, then stepped over a few paces to pick up a practice ball that had been lying there for half a game. But for game 1 of the Series the field had been covered with new sod. Each blade of grass looked as though it had been individually trimmed. "A peanut could not have been hidden there today."

A sweltering crowd of 33,242 waited impatiently for the game to begin. Many of the fans, who had seen rain clouds in the morning, had arrived wearing coats, which were now quickly peeled off under the sizzling sun. Despite the record crowd, the attendance was a trifle under expectations, with the receipts totaling $149,268—slightly less than the figures for the two home games that the Cardinals had played against the Yankees in the previous World Series.

At 11:50 a.m. a roar went up as the Cardinals, dressed in home club white uniforms, walked slowly out onto the field for batting practice. A few boos were also heard, but the cheers predominated. In the bleachers, someone with a horn kept the early crowd awake with long, unmusical blasts at infrequent intervals. Also part of the pregame entertainment were the efforts of workmen testing the public-address system. Invariably, whenever a voice over the loudspeaker would inquire, "Can you hear me out there?" the crowd roared back, "No!"

Sportsman's Park had been among the last to install a loudspeaker system. Instead, before the start of each game, a deep-voiced official would stand at home plate and call out the lineups to the press box through a megaphone. Then he would walk first to left field, then to

Sportsman's Park was bursting at the seams for the six games of the 1944 World Series. The infield, which rarely had a day off to recover during the regular season, was referred to as "the rockpile" by Cardinals shortstop Marty Marion. (National Baseball Hall of Fame Library, Cooperstown NY)

right field, and call out the lineups. Most of the day games began at 3 p.m., giving sportswriters for the afternoon papers virtually no time after the game to file their stories. To make matters worse for the press, the water cooler never really seemed to work.

Like many baseball stadiums of that era, Sportsman's Park had an odd shape dictated in large part by the layout of the surrounding neighborhood. Back in the 1920s, legendary sportswriter Red Smith, just finding his legs as a cub reporter, covered many Browns and Cardinals games for the *St. Louis Star*. He found the ballpark to have "a garish, county-fair sort of layout." Billboards in the outfield advertised such products as Ivory Soap and Philip Morris cigarettes. Nor was the ballpark kept in good repair. The wooden seats were wobbly, and so was the rickety ladder that sportswriters had to climb to get to the press box, which hung from the roof over the second deck of the stadium. And then there was the infield.

"We used to call it the rockpile," recalled Cardinals shortstop Marty Marion, one of the game's elite fielders. "They used to call me the pebble picker, because I was always picking up pebbles off of the ground and throwing them off the field so I wouldn't get a bad bounce. It was a very hard infield and the ball went through there very fast. We got used to it though. It was part of growing up."

Pavilions extended from both sides of the infield down to the foul poles—351 feet down the left field line, and 310 down the right field line, with dead center 422 feet away from the plate. The fences stood 11 ½ feet high, though the right field fence featured a 33-foot-high screen that was installed in 1929 after the Detroit Tigers hit eight home runs in four games.

On this day the ballpark was decked out in bunting. The only genuine wartime note came just before the start of the game when a massive bomber cruised overhead several times, then banked sharply, apparently to allow its occupants to catch a fleeting glimpse of the game about to be played below. Some fans remembered the moment during the previous year when a bomber swept so low over Yankee Stadium that it nearly hit a light tower—and almost gave New York mayor Fiorello La Guardia a heart attack.

Gone for the Series were the huge portraits of broadcasters Dizzy Dean and John O'Hara that usually hung over the scoreboard. They had been replaced by an advertisement for the St. Louis war chest.

The pregame ceremony was a simple one that ended quickly. "The folks of St. Louis are of the sort who like their baseball in the raw, so there was little pomp or ceremony to the launching of this third wartime World Series," Drebinger reported in the *Times*. White-haired Governor John W. Bricker of Ohio, who was the Republican vice presidential nominee that year, appeared on the field just before game time to shake hands with both managers, who happened to be Ohio natives as well. But there was to be no tossing out of the first ball. Partisan feelings about the two teams, reporters noted, seemed to be about evenly divided.

The only Browns who had ever appeared in a World Series game before 1944 were the club's three coaches: Sewell, Fred Hofmann, and Zack Taylor. If the Browns had decided to throw the dice and put long-shot Denny Galehouse on the mound, the Cardinals, in contrast, were taking no chances. The Browns would be facing Mort Cooper, probably the best pitcher in the National League, who had already won four World Series starts, including the first game of the 1942 series. When a reporter asked Cooper if he felt fit, the taciturn Missourian simply replied, "Uh huh."

Before the Series opener, the Cardinals exuded confidence, with most players telling reporters that they expected to defeat their hometown rivals in the fall just as they had in the exhibition series that spring. Pepper Martin, setting the tone for the Redbirds, opined, "I think we'll beat the hell out of the Browns. All my friendship for such pals as Don Gutteridge, Al Hollingsworth, a few others comes to an end, as of today."

With the Cardinals as the home team for the first two games, Gutteridge was first at bat for the Browns. He watched as a ball and then two strikes whizzed past him, then popped out to Marion at shortstop. Kreevich and Laabs then struck out.

Not only had Browns pitcher Denny Galehouse never appeared in a World Series game, he had never seen one either. "It's just another ball game to me," he told reporters. "I never even saw a World Series game before, because I resolved long ago that I wouldn't see one until I was in it. I never thought I'd make it, but here I am."

Whether he was as calm and collected as he pretended to be, Galehouse had no trouble getting first Cardinals batter Johnny Hopp to swing at his first pitch and fly out to Laabs in left field. He next struck out Roy Sanders on three pitches. The brass band in the stands then struck up "Take It Easy" as Stan Musial strode to the plate. He quickly got the first hit of the Series with a single up the middle, but then Walker Cooper flied out to center, with Kreevich making the final putout.

Mort Cooper continued to dominate the Browns in the second inning. Vern Stephens bounced to the pitcher for the first out. After Gene Moore walked, Cooper jammed McQuinn with an inside fastball that caused him to fly out to shallow left field. Mark Christman struck out on a called third strike.

Galehouse seemed on his way to returning the favor by retiring Kurowski and Litwhiler in quick succession. But then Marion doubled just inside the left field foul line. Verban followed with a single over second, but Gutteridge, a Cardinals castoff, was able to collar the ball behind the bag and hold Marion on third. Galehouse closed the inning by fanning Cooper.

At the top of the third, Hayworth was up first and grounded out to third. Then Galehouse fell behind on the count 0-2, but luckily drew a walk. After Cooper got Gutteridge to fly out, Kreevich bobbled one to the mound, and once again the Browns were quickly left scoreless.

The Cardinals, though, used their bottom half of the third to unleash just a fraction of their awesome power. First up was Hopp, who drilled a grounder through the hole between first and second. Sanders then powered a liner to right field that Gene Moore leaped for, momentarily seemed to catch, but could not hold onto. But the play was close enough that Hopp, holding up until he saw how the ball would be played, could only make it to second. Southworth then signaled for ace hitter Musial to execute a sacrifice bunt, which the slugger almost beat out, to put runners at second and third base with only one out. That brought up Walker Cooper, who had hit an impressive .317 in 1944, not to mention a combined .289 in his two previous Series appearances.

Musial's deft bunt under Southworth's direction was strictly according to the playbook, but now it was time for Sewell to do a little masterminding of his own. Taking no chances, he had Galehouse intentionally walk Cooper to load the bases—and also set up a potential double play. Then it was all up to Galehouse. He never faltered, fanning the long-clouting Whitey Kurowski, whose homer had sunk the Yankees in 1942, with two fouls and a fastball. Next up was Litwhiler, a fearsome power hitter—and, in fact, the only player ever to hit a ball over the double-deck left field bleachers at the Polo Grounds, where the Giants played, a distance of some 505 feet. But this time he only grounded to third baseman Mark Christman for an inning-closing force-out.

The top of the fourth seemed destined to be as anticlimactic for the Browns as the first three. Laabs flied out and Stephens hit a pop-up to Marion. But then Moore, the shopworn outfielder whom the Senators had jettisoned the previous winter, whacked a single to right field for the first ever Browns hit in a World Series. That brought up George McQuinn. The ex-seminarian's back had been bothering him late in the season, causing him to get just 10 hits in his last 60 at-bats, for a .167 average. McQuinn was shrewd enough to know, though, that he had a reputation as an opposite-field hitter. That was precisely why Cooper had thrown him the inside fastball on his first time up. This time Cooper let loose with a pitch that was low and away, outside the strike zone. McQuinn assumed that his opponent was setting him up for another inside fastball, but this time he was waiting for it and sent the ball streaking over the densely packed right field pavilion. Suddenly, the Browns had a 2 to 0 lead, and bedlam broke out in the stands.

An inspired Galehouse kept the Cardinals in check, retiring the next three batters in order. In the fifth, the Browns also went down quickly, unable to extend their lead. In the Cardinals half of the fifth, with one man on base on a walk, Musial hit into a double play to end the inning.

In the top of the sixth inning the Browns managed to get only one man on base—Vern Stephens, who got a walk with two men out.

Things got more interesting when the Cardinals came up to bat in their half of the sixth, however. Pinch-hitting for Emil Verban, Augie Bergamo led off and drew a walk. Southworth then sent in another pinch hitter, this time Debs Garms, for Mort Cooper. When Garms grounded out, Bergamo advanced to second, and for the first time since the third inning the Redbirds had a man in scoring position. But Bergamo was left stranded on base when Galehouse got Johnny Hopp to fly out to center and Ray Sanders to line out to first.

Blix Donnelly, the new pitcher for the Cardinals, wasted no time putting down the Browns in order in the eighth and ninth innings. In the bottom of the eighth, Kurowski managed to get a single for the Cardinals with two out, but was left stranded on first. Then, in the bottom of the ninth—do-or-die time—Marion, the long, lean, accomplished shortstop known affectionately as "Slats," livened up the crowd with a line drive into center field. Kreevich, diving for the ball, could not come up with it. Suddenly Marion was standing on second base—his second two-bagger of the afternoon. Bergamo then grounded out to Gutteridge, who had to range to his left to make the play, while Marion advanced to third. Southworth then sent in another pinch hitter, Ken O'Dea, who sent a towering sacrifice fly into deep center field, easily scoring Marion from third and ruining Galehouse's shutout.

Momentarily, it looked as if the big Ohio country boy might be on the ropes. But Galehouse refused to relinquish his grip, and there was to be no come-from-behind victory for the Cardinals as the Browns pitcher retired Hopp with a fly ball to Kreevich to end the game. Only fittingly, it seemed, the Browns had won their inaugural World Series game, like the real champions they were. After pausing on his way to the dugout to get a kiss from his wife, Galehouse retreated into the Browns clubhouse with the rest of his team under police escort.

Never before had a World Series game been won with such a scarcity of hits—only two. Nor had any Series pitcher ever lost on a two-hitter. The two heroes of the game, of course, were McQuinn, with his two-run homer, and Galehouse, who had pitched superbly, allowing seven hits while walking four and striking out five. As the game wore on, he had visibly gotten stronger. Five of the Cardinals' seven hits had come in the first three innings. In the ninth inning, he had thrown twenty pitches, and seventeen of those were strikes.

One of the reasons for Galehouse's success in the Series opener was summed up by catcher Red Hayworth, who said that the pitcher was throwing a fantastic "half-apple curve." The half-apple was a sweeping curveball, which broke—from twelve o'clock, near the batter's eyes, to six o'clock, below his knees—simulating half of an apple. It was Galehouse's calling card, and on this day it was the right number.

Back in the clubhouse, the gloriously happy, exultant Browns were yelling and screaming that the Series was theirs. The rooms were steaming hot with the showers going full blast, all the players were yipping and yelling, and Milt Byrnes, the alternate left fielder, was heard to cry out, "Just three more to go, boys. Just three more to go. We'll take 'em for sure."

Sewell was generous in victory, laughing off the failure of his team to get more than two hits and telling reporters, "We were lucky, we had the breaks, and I freely admit it. You have to be lucky when a pitcher holds you to two hits. But I'm proud of the game Galehouse pitched. George McQuinn's home run was really something and I'm proud of the way the entire Browns team performed." He also announced that he was starting Potter, the Browns' best pitcher, in next day's game.

The following day the *St. Louis Post-Dispatch* ran a cartoon showing a large baseball-shaped boulder labeled "Browns' momentum" rolling down a hill. At the bottom stood a worried Cardinals player, looking like he was afraid he was about to be run over. John Drebinger, in the *New York Times*, reported on an almost gleeful note that "Luke Sewell's amazing Browns, the 'Cinderella team' of nondescript castoffs which only last Sunday had bagged an American League pennant, downed Billy Southworth's supposedly all-powerful Cardinals in the opening clash of the classic."

The Empire Strikes Back

In Cairo, Illinois, during spring training, Johnny L. "Pepper" Martin, once called "the Wild Horse of the Osage," rejoined his old team, the St. Louis Cardinals, as the youngest forty-year-old player ever to don a uniform. In recent years he had been managing, with not much success, a minor-league team. He told a reporter for the *Cape Girardeau Southeast Missourian* that he was merely "holding down the fort for the ball players who are soldiers, so that when they come home the game will be alive and they can practically pick up where they left off."

Cairo (pronounced Kay-roh) was an old cotton-trading center at the confluence of the Ohio and Mississippi rivers, about sixty miles downstream from Cape Girardeau, where the Browns were working out. The only grounds that passed for a local ballpark was a place called Cotter Field, which had become something like a municipal dump and was strewn with tin cans and broken glass. The townspeople cleaned the place up and laid down fresh sod, and also transferred 700 portable seats from a high school gymnasium for the use of spectators. But the Cardinals were unable to stage anything more than intrasquad games. All the other midwestern teams—the Reds, Indians, Tigers, Cubs, and White Sox— were spread out over Indiana, while the Browns were playing the Toledo Mudhens. As a result, the Cardinals played only two real games during spring training—both against the army's Fourth Ferrying Group from Memphis, another few miles downstream.

During spring training, the only Cardinals hurler who remained a holdout was Mort Cooper, the tall right-hander whose twenty-one victories the previous year had sparked the team to their second straight National League pennant. He was also the only Cardinal to beat the Yankees in the World Series. Cooper was one of the Cardinals' two aces, the other being Max Lanier. When Cooper first came up to the majors, he was known for his fastball but nothing else. Later he developed a forkball and worked on control. Marion recalled how he often used to say, "Marty, you're my best friend. Those double plays!" In 1942, 1943, and 1944, Cooper won more than twenty games each year.

Stockily built, with short arms, Lanier had both a good curveball and a good fastball, and he was also a fair hitter. In fact, most of the Cardinal pitchers were better-than-average hitters for pitchers, including Harry Brecheen, Murry Dickson, and Johnny Beazley. Mort Cooper was even occasionally used as a pinch hitter.

Hubert Max Lanier had started out right-handed, then turned south-paw at age eight after he suffered a broken right arm when he fell off a porch. While the arm was in a sling, he began to favor the left arm. After his right arm was broken a second and then a third time, he had little choice but to throw left-handed. The Cardinals first heard of Lanier in 1938, when he was only eighteen years old, and tried to sign him to a contract. But when he learned that the team wanted to send him to the minor leagues and were offering an insignificant amount of money to boot, he declined the offer and pitched for semipro teams in North Carolina instead. Lanier pitched the Cardinals' 1944 opener in April against Pittsburgh, holding the Pirates to two singles to make his first victory a shutout, 2 to 0.

Although Mort Cooper held out for a time during spring training, his brother Walker, a catcher, signed up right away. A story told about the likable Walker dated back to the time he was with Cincinnati. During spring training, he had decided to take a cocky young kid named Ed Bailey down a notch.

"You say you're so fast," Cooper told him. "I'll race you any time for 100 yards. Ten bucks."

Bailey eagerly agreed, and both men handed over $10 to the trainer. Then Cooper said, "Wait a minute. Did I say 100? Ed, I don't think I can go 100. Make it 75, and the bet's on."

Bailey said, "Go ahead, that's fine."

They started off, and Bailey quickly went into the lead, with Cooper bouncing along far behind. Finally, after Cooper lumbered across the finish line, a distant second, Bailey said to the trainer, "Give me the money."

"No, it's not your money," the trainer told him. "It's Walker's."

Gasping for breath, Cooper explained, "Ed, we said we'd race for $10. We didn't say win. I raced you for 75 yards."

Then he told the trainer, "Give it to the clubhouse man. All right, everybody gets Cokes."

Unlike the Yankees and most other major-league clubs, the Cardinals had not seen their ranks decimated by the draft. From their 1942 championship team, five of the eight regulars and two of the best pitchers were still on hand in 1944. So were first baseman Ray Sanders; pitchers Brecheen and George Munger, who had both been rookies in 1943; and outfielder Danny Litwhiler. Johnny Hopp was moved to center field, where he was flanked by Litwhiler and Musial, Harry Walker having entered service. Whitey Kurowski, the third baseman who suffered from osteomyelitis as a child and had had a piece of bone removed from his right arm, was 4-F. His throwing arm was six inches shorter than his left arm. Walker Cooper had an old leg injury that moved him down the draft list because he could serve only in a limited capacity.

Though the Cardinals could not match the Browns or Giants in quantity of 4-F players, "they bested them in quality." Their 4-F list included Hopp (back injury), first baseman Sanders, third baseman Kurowski, catcher Ken O'Dea (hernia), rookie second baseman Emil Verban, and pitchers Cooper (old knee injury), Brecheen, and rookie sensation Ted Wilks (stomach ulcers). In addition, Marion was 4-F owing to a childhood injury that left a bone in his right leg held together by wire. Max Lanier, a seventeen-game winner in 1943, had not been drafted. Four pitchers who had been inducted were Al Brazle, Murry Dickson, Howie Krist, and Ernie White.

Despite the relative health of the Cardinals, especially in comparison to the Yankees, their archrivals in the American League, owner Sam Breadon could not resist a moment of self-pity when, during the winter of 1943–44, he told a reporter, "There isn't a club in either league which has lost as many regulars as we have." But by March he had obviously begun to realize his good fortune, boasting to another reporter, "I don't see how anybody can beat us." Dan Daniel of the *Sporting News* agreed with him, writing, "If the Cardinals are able to maintain their current lineup for even half the season, it will be downright murder."

The Cardinals had acquired left fielder Danny Litwhiler on June 1, 1943, in a trade with the Phillies, after moving Musial from left field to right. Two years earlier, Litwhiler had hit eighteen home runs, but manager Billy Southworth had been more impressed by his hustle and determination. In the last week of the 1942 season, with the Cardinals tied neck and neck with the Dodgers for the National League championship,

Cardinals owner Sam Breadon was known as a penny-pincher and was disliked by many of his players, including Stan Musial. (National Baseball Hall of Fame Library, Cooperstown NY)

the Cardinals were playing against Philadelphia. The Phillies were down one run in the ninth inning when Litwhiler went up to bat, lined the ball over the second baseman's head, then managed to stretch it into a double. When the next batter hit the ball straight to outfielder Terry Moore, Litwhiler decided to head for home. He and the ball arrived at home plate at the same time, and Litwhiler ran straight into Mort Cooper, knocking both himself and Cooper out cold. But he was safe.

"Do you know why I traded for you?" Southworth asked him, after Litwhiler arrived in St. Louis.

Billy Southworth led the Cardinals to their third straight National League pennant in 1944. (National Baseball Hall of Fame Library, Cooperstown NY)

"I have no idea, but I'm glad you did," Litwhiler replied, not altogether truthfully. Litwhiler had been brokenhearted when he heard he had been traded to St. Louis. "I felt pretty bad about it, because I really liked Philadelphia," he later recalled. "In fact, I cried. It broke my heart."

"You remember that game where you got the base hit stretching that double and scored?" Southworth reminded him.

"Yeah, I do remember."

"Anyone who can hustle on a last-place club like that would really do a first-place club a lot of good."

Like many of his teammates, Litwhiler was a great admirer of William Harrison "Billy" Southworth, a forty-eight-year-old former major-league outfielder who had first managed the Cardinals in 1929. Back then, his sub-.500 record had quickly earned him a sojourn in the minor leagues. In 1940 he was given a second chance to manage the Cardinals, and this time he took a sixth-place team and guided it to a third-place finish. Southworth liked to keep an alarm clock on the field during spring training. For fifteen minutes at a time, he would order his team to go through each of the fundamentals—especially how to bunt and how to slide. Except for Musial, the Cardinals did not have many power hitters, nor was Southworth eager for his men to hit home runs. He preferred that they go for the extra base.

When Litwhiler joined the Cardinals in 1943, he was hired at $8,000 a year. The highest-paid player on the club was Marty Marion at $12,000. The Coopers each were receiving $10,000, and Musial $9,000. Everybody thought the Marions were rich because they had bought a car, something Musial still could not afford.

Despite his youth, Musial was a natural leader, never getting into arguments with his teammates but silently going about getting the job done. Once, after he hit a home run, someone called out, "Nice going, Stan. What is that, your fourteenth or fifteenth?" Musial replied, "I don't know. I'll hit them. You count them."

Unlike the fractious Browns, whose every other player seemed a loner, a drinker, or a brawler, the Cardinals enjoyed each other's company to a considerable degree, and many were family men as well. St. Louis was, and is, a notoriously humid city, and after a home night game many of the players liked to head down to the Ozarks for a day or two of relaxation. The area was as big as the state of Maine, with numerous woods, streams, lakes, and giant springs. Litwhiler had a friend who owned a cabin on a lake, and on most days off during the summer many of the players and their families would go there to relax.

Particularly after a night game, Musial and Brecheen enjoyed going out on the lake and gigging frogs, staying out until two, three, or even four in the morning. On their return, they barbecued them. Finally, in the cool of the morning they were able to fall asleep.

How hot was it in St. Louis during July and August? Dodger outfielder

Billy Herman remembered it this way, recalling the train route that went from Chicago to St. Louis to Cincinnati:

> You got on a train at midnight, and maybe that train had been sitting in the yards all day long, under a broiling sun. It feels like 150 degrees in that steel car. You get into St. Louis at 6:30 in the morning, grab your own bag, fight to get a cab, and go to the hotel. By the time you get to the hotel, it's 7:30, and you have an afternoon ball game to play. So you hurry into the dining room and it's hot in there, no air-conditioning, and you eat and run upstairs to try and get a few hours' rest. Then you go to the ballpark, where it's about 110 degrees. You finish the ball game around 5 or 5:30, and go into the clubhouse. It's around 120 degrees in there. You take your shower, but there's no way you can dry off. The sweat just keeps running off of you. You go out to the street and try to find a cab back to the hotel. You get back to the hotel and go up to your room and you lose your breath, it's so hot in there. But the dining room isn't much better, so you order room service and stay right there and eat. Then you go to bed and try to sleep, but you can't, you're sweating so much. So you get up and pull the sheet off the bed and soak it with cold water and go back and roll up in a wet sheet. But it dries out after an hour or two, and you have to get up and soak it again. This goes on for four days in St. Louis, and you go on to Cincinnati and it's the same thing.

At the time, many baseball clubs were providing beer to players in the clubhouse after a game. But the Cardinals were still a dry team. One day a group of players said to Southworth, "Hey, Billy, how about getting us some beer in the clubhouse."

"Nah, I don't know," he replied. Finally, though, he consented.

Soon afterward, the team was in Brooklyn for a twilight doubleheader. The Cardinals won the first game and had a little downtime.

"Okay, can we have beer in the clubhouse?" the players asked Southworth.

The beer was brought out, and Kurowski and another player had a beer. Then the Cardinals lost the second game.

"Okay, no more beer in the clubhouse from now on," Southworth announced after the game, and that was that.

The Cardinals also had a winning spirit and a winning attitude that was unique. As Litwhiler later recalled, that was the difference between the Cardinals and any other team he ever played with. "You knew you were going to win. Every day you knew you were going to win. And if you lost, it was 'Okay, we'll win tomorrow.' And it didn't really bother you. And you usually won the next day."

In 1944 the Brooklyn Dodgers were thought to be the Cardinals' chief rivals. But their ranks had been decimated. Dolph Camilli, Billy Herman, Arky Vaughan, and Kirby Higbe had all gone into the service. Whitlow Wyatt, suffering from a sore arm, quit in midseason. The other contender, Cincinnati, also lost its two best pitchers in 1944—Johnny Vander Meer and Elmer Riddle.

Not surprisingly, the Cardinals launched their 1944 season with one of the best starts ever in the National League, winning 45 of their first 60 games, then winning 60 of the next 94, to finish the season with a 105-49 record.

"Common sense had to tell you the competition wasn't as good as it was before," Marion remembered. "But as a player, you don't notice that sort of thing at all. I don't ever remember playing a game where we said, 'I wish we had Enos and Terry.' We just played the game like that was it. We never mentioned the war. You put out nine players, we put out nine players, and we play."

On offense, first baseman Ray Sanders led off, and in 1944 was to drive in 102 runs. He was followed by Kurowski, the third baseman, who hit 20 home runs and drove in 87 runs. Musial, who batted third, hit .347 and drove in 97 runs. Litwhiler, another slugger, hit 15 home runs and drove in 82 runs.

The pitching staff was equally superb, leading the league in winning percentage, strikeouts, shutouts, and ERAs. Cooper, with a 2.46 ERA, won 22 games. Lanier won 17 with a 2.65 ERA, rookie Ted Wilks produced a 17-4 record with a 2.65 ERA, and Harry Brecheen won 16 games with a 2.85 ERA. A left-handed screwball pitcher, Brecheen was known as "the Cat" because, according to Marion, "he was sneaky fast," with a good change of pace. The Cardinals staff recorded 26 shutouts and had an astounding team ERA of 2.67.

Litwhiler later remembered that Southworth was a tough manager to play for because, like Sewell, he liked to play hunches. "He would pick up the ball for the pitchers during batting practices," Litwhiler recalled, "and he'd watch you hit, and if you looked good, you'd be in the lineup. If you didn't swing good, you might not be in the lineup."

One player that Southworth often used as a substitute was Martin, who though old for a ballplayer was still strong and agile. A favorite trick he used to impress his teammates with was to lay two traveling trunks side by side and then jump over them without a run. Then he would put one on top of the other and jump onto the top of them, again without a run.

By late spring 1944 the Cardinals were already leading the National League, while the rest of the standings were somewhat skewed. The Philadelphia Phillies won five straight in early May to claim second place. Charlie Grimes was brought in from Milwaukee to manage the Cubs after they lost thirteen straight.

By September 1, a month before the season ended, the Cardinals had already racked up 91 victories, or more than the Browns were to achieve for the entire season, though Pittsburgh under Frankie Frisch was a close second with 90. Yet Pittsburgh did not win another game that season, while the Cardinals won 14 more, for a winning margin of 14 ½ games. Virtually in a league of their own, they were never threatened even once by their rivals in the National League.

For the 1944 season, the Cardinals led the league in hits, runs, batting average, doubles, and home runs. Musial hit .347, Hopp .336, and Cooper .317. Even though they dozed through a long losing streak in September, the team still finished with a .682 winning percentage. Under Marion's fielding leadership, the Cardinals also made only 112 errors, the fewest in the league, and 162 double plays, the most in the league.

In doing so, the Cardinals became the first team in National League history to win a hundred games in three consecutive seasons, 1942 through 1944. Even though they do not receive the glory and recognition they deserved, because of the war, the Cardinals in those three years were the most dominant team in National League history.

The Browns and Cardinals players did not know one another well at all. When one team was at home, the other was on the road, and they got together only for exhibition games during spring training. As a result, the teams never got to see one another play against a league competitor. But they did follow each other's progress, especially during the 1944 season. As the Series approached, the Cardinals as a club had little doubt that they could vanquish their hometown rivals. "But after we played them that first game, we changed our minds," Marion recalled. "Hey, they were a pretty good ball club."

Musial agreed with Marion's assessment of the Browns: "Everybody thought we had a better club, and we did, too, but that was one of the toughest Series we played. They played tough, and we were always having to play catch-up. We had a hard time winning against the Browns. They had Galehouse, Potter had that screwball, and Jack Kramer and Jakucki." What surprised Musial was that during the Series the fans were rooting for the Browns. "The fans were rooting for the underdog, and I was surprised about that, but after you analyze the situation in St. Louis, the Browns in the good old days had good clubs. They had great players like George Sisler and Kenny Williams, and the fans who were there were older fans, older men, old-time Brownie fans. But it was a tough Series."

Throughout the entire Series, Marion recalled,

> I guarantee ya, you couldn't even see that damn baseball in that ballpark. They had people sitting in the center field bleachers, all those white shirts out there. I never saw such a horrible background in a ballpark. You could hardly see the ball. A lot of sunshine, a lot of bright shirts, in the field even getting the ball off the bat was very difficult to see. A lot of white shirts. And very glary. And a lot of sunshine, particularly when you were hitting. The pitching wasn't that good, even though the hitting was horrible. We always claimed that we couldn't see the damn ball.

Musial seconded Marion's complaint. Years later, in his autobiography, Musial commented, "The background at Sportsman's Park made batting difficult whenever a white-shirted crowd jammed into the center field bleachers. . . . A couple of years later I helped persuade Sam Breadon to rope off the center field section of the bleachers. Subsequently, [future Cardinals owner] Gussie Busch turned that vacated area into an arboretum that improved the appearance of the ball park and helped the hitters even more."

During the Series, neither Southworth nor any of the players knew that Marion was suffering from the flu and playing with a temperature of 104. At the same time, his wife was giving birth to their second child. As soon as a game was over, Marion headed back to his room at the Melbourne Hotel, and for three days the only nourishment he took was orange juice. In the morning, after drinking his juice, he went to the ballpark, feeling "as weak as hell," as he later described it. "Nobody knew I was sick. I had a temperature the whole Series, taking medicine and drinking orange juice. But I played all right. I didn't play great, but I played all right."

Born in Richburg, South Carolina, Martin Whitford Marion had grown up in Atlanta but made St. Louis his home after his rookie season

Marty Marion was named the Most Valuable Player in the National League in 1944. (National Baseball Hall of Fame Library, Cooperstown NY)

in 1940. Articulate and hard-nosed, he was able to distinguish himself financially at a time when most players had little leverage. Early in his career he had been saddled with a great-field, no-hit label, but he eventually overcame that reputation to hit a league-leading thirty-six doubles in 1942. His career average was .263.

Marion's easygoing nature and sense of humor sometimes got him into trouble. Once he was at bat facing Brooklyn's Whit Wyatt, a fierce and

Walker Cooper, left, and his brother Mort were major factors in the Cardinals' stellar 1944 season. (National Baseball Hall of Fame Library, Cooperstown NY)

occasionally dirty competitor. Taking his time securing a foothold at the plate, Marion looked out and saw Wyatt glaring back at him.

"You ready?" the pitcher called out, and then promptly knocked Marion down with his first pitch.

Marion got up, laughing, and with his next pitch Wyatt hit him in the ribcage.

"Jesus Christ, Whit!" Marion yelled.

"Don't laugh at me when I'm on the mound," Wyatt replied.

Walker Cooper was the club prankster, giving hotfoots with wooden matches or crushing straw hats, though his favorite trick was to sit in a hotel lobby and set his newspaper on fire. Unlike other catchers, who used a sponge or handkerchief in his mitt, Walker preferred a woman's falsie.

Happy-go-lucky Walker's older brother, Mort, was just the opposite. A no-nonsense pitcher, he chewed aspirin while on the mound to deaden the pain in the elbow of his pitching arm caused by bone chips.

During the season, Pepper Martin hit .279 in twenty-nine games and helped keep the club loose with his sense of humor. Once, when Musial lost a high fly ball in bright sunlight, the ball glanced off his head and right into Martin's glove. After firing the ball to the relay man in the infield, Martin called time to see if his teammate was all right, then gently inquired, "Mind if I laugh?"

"Not all all," an embarrassed Musial replied.

Martin then dropped his glove, fell down on the grass, and howled until the umpire strode out to see what was going on.

Over the course of the 1944 season, Breadon was no doubt pleased that the Brooklyn Dodgers, now under the generalship of his former employee Branch Rickey, were struggling. But he was worried by the rising fortunes of his landlord, the St. Louis Browns, whose attendance was increasing at the end of the season as they battled the Yankees and Tigers for the flag. After all the hard work and money he had poured into his club to make it the city's best, suddenly it all seemed for nothing if the Browns were to shed their "lovable losers" image and become the "Cinderella team" of all time. Making matters worse, gate receipts were in sharp decline, thanks to the lack of a serious rival in the National League. Many if not most fans probably did not expect the Browns to duplicate their stunning success in beating the Yankees by winning the World Series, but surely sentiment was on their side.

Perhaps that was why Nelson Potter decided, on the morning of game 2, to shave. The Browns starter had a superstition about not shaving on a day when he was pitching, but on this day he decided to take the mound clean-shaven. He may also have been feeling not just confident but lucky after the St. Louis Beer Company gave him and each of his teammates a silver horseshoe to hang over their lockers.

Sitting in the stands, enjoying the second game of the all–St. Louis Series, was Harry S. Truman. The Missouri senator was also the Democratic Party's vice presidential nominee that year, running on the ticket with incumbent Franklin Delano Roosevelt. In only seven months, he would assume the presidency upon FDR's death.

In the first inning, leadoff hitter Don Gutteridge went down swinging. Marion then made a great stop near second base to toss out Kreevich. Laabs ended the inning by sending a towering fly to Hopp in center field.

Marion's incredible sleight-of-hand feats at shortstop were the talk of the afternoon. "I even surprised myself," he smilingly admitted afterward. "Since they resodded the infield, I never thought I'd be able to catch a ball. You see, I'm used to nothing but bad bounces."

Bergamo was first man up for the Cardinals. With the count 3-2, he fouled out to Hayworth near the plate. Kreevich then made a running catch of Hopp's fly in short center, and Potter closed the inning by striking out Musial.

Marion then threw out Stephens, who led off the second inning for the Browns. McQuinn fouled off the first pitch, then walked on four straight balls. Christman went down swinging, and Moore also fanned. Walker Cooper led off the bottom of the second inning with a single that turned into a double after his line drive took a freak bounce over Chet Laabs's head. It was the first bad bounce the Browns had to contend with. Unfazed, Potter struck out Kurowski, though Cooper moved to third. Christman then took Marion's grounder to third base and tossed him out.

The Browns' half of the third was much like the first two innings. Marion went far back on the grass to take Hayworth's high fly. Potter was next up and hit to Marion, who easily threw him out. Gutteridge walked, but Kreevich hit to Marion, who threw to Verban at second base to retire the side.

In the bottom of the third, Verban led off by rapping a single. Lanier then bunted, popping the ball high into the air. Slow off the mound, Potter was unable to make the catch and let the ball bounce. Instead of allowing third baseman Mark Christman to scoop the ball and throw to first, he picked it up himself and, without getting a firm grip on it, pivoted and threw to first. But the throw was wide of the bag. Second baseman Gutteridge, covering at first, tried to stretch for the ball, but it sailed over his head and into right field. Verban landed on third. Next up was Bergamo, who hit a soft bouncer, scoring Verban. It was the first run scored against Potter in twenty-two innings, or since September 21. Yet he was to blame for the run and was charged with two errors.

"The mishandled bunt was an oddity in itself," Daley observed in the *New York Times*. "Lanier popped up ingloriously but the ball squirted

Second baseman Don Gutteridge was a nondrinker who could be relied on to keep some of his Browns teammates out of trouble. (National Baseball Hall of Fame Library, Cooperstown NY)

down at Potter's feet, with Red Hayworth and Mark Christman also lunging for it. The pitcher pounced on it and uncorked an inelegant heave into right field as Emil Verban aced to third and eventually completed his journey."

What made the play even more fantastic, Daley noted, was that Potter had equaled a World Series record. Never had a pitcher made more than two errors in a Series, but Potter had managed to come up with two on the same play. "The giddy Browns never do things by halves. It's whole loaf or none with them."

In the fourth inning, a rare fielding lapse by Browns third baseman Mark Christman put the Cardinals up by another run. With one out and runners on first and second, Marion hit a double play grounder to third. But Christman, too eager to make the play before he had secured the ball in his glove, botched it, and the ball went careening into foul territory behind the bag. The runners were all safe on the error. Verban than knocked a fly ball into left. Sanders, on third, barely beat Laabs's throw home to give the Cardinals a 2 to 0 lead.

Gene Moore, who had gotten the first Browns hit in game 1, did an encore in game 2. Leading off for the Browns in the fifth, he punched a bunt to the right side of the infield and past Lanier. Though Verban got to the ball, it was not in time to catch Moore. However, the Browns failed to cash in.

The Browns did not get another hit until the seventh inning, with two out, when Moore again singled, this time a sharp drive to center field. Hayworth followed with a long double to left center field to score Moore and cut the lead to 2 to 1. Sewell then sent Mancuso in to pinch-hit for Potter, and Mancuso delivered a single to center, scoring Hayworth to tie the game.

In the eighth inning, with the score still tied 2 to 2, Kreevich led off with a double off the left field wall. Lanier had been suffering from a sore elbow and had not pitched a game since September 22, having lost seven straight decisions, so Southworth now decided to go to his bullpen.

George Byerly had been warming up, and most fans and sportswriters expected that he would get the call to come in as the reliever. But out on the mound, Marion persuaded Southworth not to use the stronger, bigger pitcher.

"Byerly has a bad leg," Marion reminded Southworth. "And Billy, the Browns will try to bunt that run over to *third*. Byerly won't be able to handle the bunt. Bring in Donnelly."

Cardinals relief pitcher Blix Donnelly was born Sylvester Ulysses Donnelly. "You can see why they call him 'Blix,' " Bob Broeg slyly explained to his Marine readers in *Leatherneck*. Donnelly himself had no idea what his nickname meant, remembering only that his father had given it to him.

Unlike most pitchers, who tended to be slender and tall, Donnelly

Sylvester "Blix" Donnelly's standout pitching and fielding helped the National League champions to even the World Series at one game apiece. (National Baseball Hall of Fame Library, Cooperstown NY)

was short and chunky, weighing 175 pounds and measuring just five foot nine. He was also, at twenty-nine, the low man on the Cardinals' pitching totem pole. This was his first full season with the Redbirds, though he had put in a lengthy apprenticeship in the minor leagues, chalking up outstanding records in Springfield, Missouri; Sacramento, California; and Rochester, New York—including three no-hitters. But as a Cardinal, he had pitched fewer innings and won fewer games (only two) than any of his teammates.

Donnelly had been fighting the cynics about his small stature his entire professional life. Back in 1938 he had been sent by the Cardinals to a franchise team in Decatur, Illinois, where the coach, a man named Tony Kaufmann, told him, "Kid, you'll never make it. You're too small." Disgusted by the lack of confidence in his abilities, Donnelly asked then Cardinals general manager Branch Rickey to send him somewhere else. Rickey obliged by dispatching Donnelly to the Daytona Beach team in the Florida League, and then to Springfield in the Western Association. The Springfield team's attempt to sell Donnelly to the Fort Worth Cats in the Texas League fell through when Donnelly came down with malaria, even though the pitcher was being offered for only $300.

"I realize it's asking too much for you to gamble a huge sum like $300 on me," Donnelly sarcastically remarked to Cecil Coombs, the manager of the Cats, "but would you please tell me why?"

"My boy," came the reply, as Coombs puffed on his cigar, "you're too small."

Donnelly got so mad that he went out and won nineteen of his first twenty games for Springfield.

So it was not surprising that Donnelly was still angry when he took the mound for his Series debut. As he later told the *Sporting News*, "I was ripping mad because I wanted to show Billy Southworth that I could pitch like that. Nobody ever has believed I can. They take one look at me and say, with a compassionate look, 'Too bad he's so small.'" He was plain tired, he added, of being ignored while everyone doted on the "big bohunks who haven't half the stuff I have on the ball."

Donnelly had a history of being a strikeout pitcher, whiffing 304 batters in 271 innings in the minors back in 1941. After he had taken his five warm-up pitches, Laabs, the hero of the final game of the season against the Yankees, stepped up to the plate. This time, however, Laabs was not to duplicate his heroic feat or anything like it, striking out, as the *St. Louis Post-Dispatch* reported, "as though trying to swat butterflies with a pipe cleaner." Donnelly next struck out Stephens and intentionally walked McQuinn. Then Christman went down swinging to end the threat.

At the end of nine innings, the game was still tied. After a scoreless tenth, McQuinn started off the top of the eleventh by almost hitting his second homer of the Series, but the ball bounced off the right field pavilion screen for an automatic double. Next up was Christman, who bunted down the third base line, perhaps just a bit too hard. Donnelly pounced off the mound, picked up the ball, quickly spun around, and threw to Kurowski at third. The throw beat McQuinn, who was called out.

Donnelly's "astoundingly executed play" made all the difference between victory and defeat, Daley wrote in the *Times*. Kurowski also had to make a phenomenal catch and "an even more phenomenal stab at the sliding McQuinn. This was the same Kurowski, by the way, who was knocked bowlegged by Johnny Lindell of the Yankees in a similar crucial turning point a year ago. But McQuinn was more polite. He didn't ruffle Whitey's hair. And that meant the ball game."

In the bottom of the inning, Sanders led off with a single against Muncrief, who had come into the game after Potter was replaced by a pinch hitter in the seventh. Kurowski moved Sanders to second with a sacrifice bunt. Then Marty Marion was intentionally walked to set up the double play. Southworth sent backup catcher Ken O'Dea, the Cardinals' top pinch hitter, to bat for Verban. "Though not a consistent hitter," the World Series program noted, "he has swat many timely wallops to turn defeats into victories."

Living up to that reputation, O'Dea singled to right to score Sanders with the winning run, and bring his own World Series career average to .500 (6 for 12) in five games.

The Browns had simply run out of miracles, John Drebinger reported in the *New York Times*. "The big fellow of this all–St. Louis World Series finally caught up with the little fellow and deftly put him in his place." As for Donnelly, he had "revealed himself to be one more of those amazingly effective rookie pitchers."

That eighth inning, Broeg wrote, "was the frame that really balanced the Series in favor of the Cardinals, though the game wasn't terminated until the eleventh." "Blix," said Broeg, "had blitzed the Browns for good back in the eighth."

Though the Browns lost, pitchers Nelson Potter and Bob Muncrief had put in an effort that very nearly rivaled Donnelly's. Both of the Cardinals' runs, in the third and fourth innings, were unearned and attributable to the Browns' four errors. The game was the first World Series contest to go into extra innings since the fourth and last game of the 1939 championship, when the Yankees downed Cincinnati in ten innings. Catcher Walker Cooper also went into the record books with fifteen putouts, another high for a World Series game.

"The witching hour finally struck for the Cinderella Brownies," Arthur Daley wrote in the *New York Times*. Square-jawed Irishman Ken O'Dea finally broke Sewell's uncanny magic spell. "But it was a mighty close call."

A different perspective was offered by Sewell's mother, up from Alabama to watch her first professional baseball game. When the Browns manager finally got back to his apartment that night, he found her waiting up for him in a rocking chair.

"What did you think of the game, mom?" the manager asked her.

"Oh," she replied, "I was awfully glad when someone won. I was getting awfully tired."

Young Man Musial

The St. Louis Cardinals were a penny-pinching team under owner Sam Breadon, though many of the players blamed his general manager, Branch Rickey. After Rickey departed for the Brooklyn Dodgers, the conventional wisdom was that, financially speaking, things might get a little better. Conventional wisdom was wrong. As World War II dragged on and attendance at the Cardinals' games dwindled, Breadon tightened the screws. When the team's undisputed star, Stan Musial, returned to his hometown of Donora, Pennsylvania, at the end of the 1942 season, he was making so little money that he had to take a job working in the zinc mills. That season he had been named rookie of the year, batting .315.

During the winter, Musial tried to negotiate a raise, asking for an increase to $10,000 over his 1941 salary of $4,200. With the assistance of a Monongahela auto dealer, he wrote a letter outlining his reasons. For starters, he noted that, with Enos Slaughter and Terry Moore in the service, he was now the senior Cardinals outfielder, despite being only twenty-one years old. That meant he would have to play "even harder."

Taking a tough line, Breadon replied, "You will have no more to do this year than you did last year. I thought you were the kind of ball player that gave all you had in every game. Of course, we expect the same in 1943, if you sign a contract with us." Breadon offered Musial a raise of $1,000, while adding a take-it-or-leave-it clause. If Musial did not take the offer, he could sit out the season. When Musial balked, Breadon told him that "no one in our organization has been advanced faster than you have. We have had great outfielders on our ball club, including . . . Moore and Slaughter, and none of them in their second year received a contract for as much as $5,500."

Musial replied that comparison with such Depression-era salaries was

Stan Musial, just twenty-three in 1944, was already a superstar and a potent hitter. He batted .347 during the regular season and .204 in the World Series. (National Baseball Hall of Fame Library, Cooperstown NY)

meaningless in an age of higher taxes and inflation. Breadon was not persuaded, and suggested that his star outfielder come to St. Louis to discuss the matter further. If he chose to sit out the 1943 season, the ball club would pay for his round-trip expenses. Musial decided to reject the offer and did not report for spring training. Breadon then dispatched farm director Eddie Dyer to Donora to sign up Musial for the season for $6,250. Rickey, of course, would have shown the young Pennsylvanian no

In 1944 Stan Musial led the league in hits, slugging percentage, and on-base percentage, helping the Cardinals to 105 victories. (National Baseball Hall of Fame Library, Cooperstown NY)

such mercy. With the auto dealer, his friend and adviser, out of town, an anxious Musial signed. Though he was never to feel any warmth toward Breadon, he remained the consummate team player. Throughout his career Musial avoided public controversy and quietly went about doing his job.

Stanley Frank Musial had grown up in Donora, a bleak mill town of about 15,000 on the banks of the Monongahela River and just downwind about twenty-eight miles from Pittsburgh's steel mills. The grass, "stained by perennial smog," was never very green, according to one of Musial's biographers, while the skies were "often blacker than the inside of an umpire's pockets." The town's frame houses were covered with decades of smoke and ash from the blast furnaces, the galvanizing mills, and the zinc plant, built in 1915. Sulphur and chemical fumes had laid bare the hills and surrounding countryside. Most of the town's inhabitants were immigrants from Poland, Czechoslovakia, Russia, and Germany.

Mary Lancos, Musial's mother, was born in New York City, one of nine children; her parents were of Czech descent. The family later moved to

Donora, and by age eight Mary was earning extra money for the family by working as a house cleaner. "As a teenager, she rowed her coal-mining father across the Monongahela River so he could work deep within the bowels of the earth for 90 cents a day." Later she went to work sorting nails at the American Steel and Wire Company, which was to Donora what General Motors was to Detroit, and there she met a wiry young Pole named Lukasz Musial, four years her senior, who had been born in Warsaw. At the time, Lukasz was working in the company's shipping department, where he earned $11 every two weeks lifting hundred-pound bales of wire. They married two years later, when Mary was seventeen. Four girls—Ida, Helen, Victoria, and Rose—were born before Stanislaus arrived on November 21, 1920. He was immediately nicknamed Stashu, a name later Americanized to Stanley. Lukasz was so eager for another son that he vowed not to have Stanislaus baptized until another one came along. Two years later, when Edward was born, both boys were baptized on the same day in a Catholic ceremony. Later the family moved to an unpretentious house on Marelda Avenue that had belonged to Mary Musial's grandmother.

On weekends, Stan sometimes accompanied his father and brother to the local Polish National Alliance gymnasium, where tumbling was popular. At Donora High School, Musial excelled at both basketball and baseball, though both parents wanted their son to go to college to escape working in the mines and mills. Occasionally, he hung out with a neighbor named Joe Barbao, a former minor-league pitcher who still played semipro ball and worked in the zinc mill as a short shifter—"a job so brutal no one worked more than three hours a day because of the intense heat." Barbao also managed a local semipro team, the Donora Zincs, and often recruited Musial as a batboy when the team was playing at nearby Palmer Park. Under Barbao's tutelage, Musial soon became proficient enough to play ball with older boys, and at age fourteen he joined the Heslep All-Stars, a junior city-league team. In a game against Cement City, he struck out fourteen batters and walked two in a 24 to 2 win. He was only fifteen when Barbao invited the young southpaw to pitch against a hard-hitting team from nearby Monessen. Musial pitched six innings and struck out thirteen players, all adults.

While playing with the Zincs, Musial could not help noticing that the right field fence, the natural target of a left-handed batter like himself, was significantly farther away than the fence in left field. As a result, he practiced reaching out and knocking the ball past the third baseman.

Even as a teenager, Musial showed the majestic might he was later to display as a future Hall of Famer. He remembered a Donora High School game against a team from Monongahela City: "My brother Ed, a ninth-grader who was playing the outfield for us, walked to fill the bases in the late inning of a game we were losing. I was up next. The Mon City pitcher, a right-hander named Jack McGinty, threw me a fast ball low and inside. Unlike most young players, I was a good low-ball hitter. I hit the ball so far, about 450 feet against the distant right field fence on one bounce, that I had circled the bases before the ball was touched by the retrieving outfielder." In his senior year Musial also led his high school basketball team to an undefeated season.

After high school, Musial turned down a basketball scholarship to the University of Pittsburgh, despite the urging of both his father and the athletic director of the high school, and signed a contract with the St. Louis Cardinals' Monessen farm club. In the beginning, Musial was assigned to one of the Class D teams, playing for $65 a month while still hoping to play for the Pittsburgh Pirates—his "home team." A scouting report dated June 5, 1937, that was sent to the Cardinals' front office noted: "Arm? Good. Fielding? Good. Speed? Fast. Good curve ball. Green kid. Prospect now? No. Prospect later? Yes. Aggressive? Yes. Habits? Good. Health? Good."

Musial spent the summer of 1937 playing ball and earning extra money pumping gas at a service station. That summer Andrew J. French, the business manager of the Monessen farm club, and Monessen manager Ollie Vanek visited Musial's father, Lukasz, and tried to persuade him to allow his son to sign a professional contract. Lukasz, who still wanted Stan to attend college and knew that the average boy's chances of success in the major leagues were minimal, refused. Young Stan, hearing his father's decision, burst into tears, but at that point his mother took matters into her own hands.

"Lukasz," Mary asked her husband, "why did you come to America?"

"Why?" he replied, caught by surprise. "Because it's a free country, that's why."

"That's right, Lukasz. And in America, a boy is free not to go to college, too."

Musial's father reluctantly gave in, and Stan and both his parents signed the contract, though it was not filed with the baseball commissioner's office until June of the following year. The previous winter young Stan had begun dating Lillian Labash, his future wife, who was a fellow student at Donora High School. The school's athletic director, James K. Russell, had been pressuring young Musial to accept the basketball scholarship to the University of Pittsburgh and give up his ambition to be a baseball player. Privately, he approached Lillian and asked her to help persuade the boy to do as his father wished and pursue a college education. She replied that the decision was Stan's, and his alone.

Even more pressure came from Musial's gym teacher, Jerry Wunderlich, who took him to the University of Pittsburgh and introduced him to Dr. H. C. Carlson, the basketball coach who had tendered the scholarship. Carlson not only repeated his offer but darkly suggested that Musial's path to baseball would probably only lead down into the dreary lower ranks of the minor leagues, where more likely than not he would get injured. The only alternative left to him then would be a job back in Donora working at the mill.

Beset by so much pressure from his father, his high school coach, and the university recruiter, Musial sought the advice of the one person at Donora High School whom he thought he could trust—Miss Helen Kloz, the librarian. When he asked her what he should do, she replied: "Stan, I've never known a boy who wanted something more than you do. College is a wise course for a man to follow, but you've got to want it enough, almost as much as you want baseball. If you're going to try baseball, the younger you start, the better. You can't afford to lose your head, but you can afford to follow your heart."

Not long afterward, Musial and a man named Johnny Bunardzya, the sports editor of the *Donora Herald-American*, drove to Pittsburgh to watch the Pirates play the New York Giants. Unaware that Musial had already signed a contract with the Cardinals, Bunardzya tried to persuade his young companion to sign with the Pirates, who were, after all, the boy's favorite team. Musial had never seen a major-league ballgame before and was amazed at what he saw, brashly confiding to Bunardzya, "John, I think I can hit big-league pitching."

During this period, the Cardinals got into trouble with the baseball commissioner's office by controlling two or more clubs in the same minor league. Kenesaw Mountain Landis ordered the Redbirds to release ninety-one ballplayers immediately. Musial, who had not yet been informed about where he was to report, began to hope that he might be one of the players released, especially after a local businessman, Irv Weiss, offered to drive him to Pittsburgh to work out with the Pirates. Letters of interest had also arrived from the New York Yankees and the

Cleveland Indians. Weiss and Musial subsequently drove to Pittsburgh, where manager Pie Traynor watched Musial work out. Later he took the young man aside and said he would like to offer him a minor-league contract. Musial then revealed that he was already under contract with the Cardinals, but added that he hoped the St. Louis team had forgotten about him.

"I doubt that, son," Traynor replied. "You'll be hearing from them one of these days. If they do release you, let us know."

A few days later, Musial received a telegram from the Cardinals front office. Musial's hands shook when he opened the envelope and read that he was to report to Williamson, West Virginia, where he would begin playing ball in the Class D Mountain League. He was to leave immediately.

In his first three seasons in the minors, Musial failed to impress anyone. Later sent to Daytona Beach in the Florida State League, he was shifted to the outfield and began to show some power as a hitter. In 1941 he moved to Springfield, and then Rochester. After Slaughter, the Cardinals' workhorse, injured himself, and the team needed another left-handed batter for their pennant drive, Musial was finally called up to the big leagues.

Musial reported to the Cardinals on September 17, 1941, just in time for a doubleheader the Cardinals were playing with the Boston Braves at Sportsman's Park.

Between games, Musial shagged flies in the outfield and took the measure of the stadium. The Cardinals readily won the first game, and Southworth decided Musial would make his major-league debut in the second. There seemed little chance he would permanently replace any of the three stellar regulars—Slaughter, Moore, and Hopp—but was merely giving "Country" Slaughter a few much-needed days off. In the first inning, after Musial left the on-deck circle, he found himself facing knuckleballer Jim Tobin. As he assumed his familiar, hip-swinging crouch, the fans tittered. The result was anticlimactic: Musial popped up to third baseman Sibby Sisti to end the inning. "Red-faced and embarrassed, the rookie tossed his bat aside and trotted out to right field as his new teammates, in the time-honored tradition of baseball, razzed him unmercifully from the dugout."

In the third inning, Musial came up to the plate for the second time, and Boston catcher Ray Berres went out to the mound to confer with Tobin on how to pitch to the newcomer. The first pitch was a ball. Musial sent the second one banging against the wall in right center field for his first major-league hit, a two-run double. Most of his teammates made a show of ignoring him, but he finished the game with a two-for-four performance. It was his double that gave the team a 3 to 2 victory. In its report on the game, the Associated Press mistakenly identified Musial as "Steve."

If 1941 was the year Ted Williams and Joe DiMaggio were making baseball history, it was also the year Musial began—from the very beginning—to rewrite the record book as well. In 12 games, he smashed 20 hits and batted .426, though that was not enough to wrest the pennant from the Dodgers. Cardinals slugger Johnny Mize later fumed that if general manager Rickey had brought up Musial sooner, "We might have gone ahead and won the pennant." He was probably right.

When Musial returned to his hometown of Donora that fall, the Donora Zinc Works Association honored him with a banquet at which he was presented with a watch and a trophy. Joe Barbao, his old friend, was master of ceremonies, and sitting at one of the banquet tables was one of baseball's immortals, Honus Wagner, a native Pennsylvanian. "Even in my most fanciful dreams," Musial later recounted in his autobiography, "I never would have dared imagine that I would play long enough and hit well enough to break many of old Honus' National League records."

By 1943 Musial had blossomed, getting 220 hits and winning the batting championship with a .357 average. He had also married his high school sweetheart, Lillian, with whom he was to have four children. His teammate Marty Marion remembered Musial as "a good ol' country boy. We had a lot of good ol' country boys on our team. Naturally, it didn't take Stan long to become famous. He was the topic of conversation because of his stance. Everyone asked, 'How can he hit with that stance?' curled up like a corkscrew at bat, and all the time he was whacking the ball all over the place. No, if you don't like Stan, you don't like anybody."

Musial was a good fastball hitter and had the feeling that "nobody could throw that fastball by me," as he later recalled. "After they found out I could hit the fastball, they started throwing more curves, and they found out I could hit the curve as well."

Asked once about the secret of his batting prowess, Musial replied, "I consciously memorized the speed at which every pitcher in the league threw his fastball, curve, and slider; then, I'd pick up the speed of the ball in the first 30 feet of its flight and knew how it would move once it had crossed the plate." Implicitly agreeing with that assessment was

Brooklyn Dodgers pitcher Carl Erskine, who once humorously described his strategy in pitching to Musial: "I've had pretty good success with Stan by throwing him my best pitch and then backing up third."

One time Marty Marion asked him, "Stan, how does the ball look to you? It looks like an aspirin tablet to me."

"It looks like a grapefruit," Musial replied, and Marion knew he was not exaggerating.

Marion also remembered that Musial "didn't have a good arm, but he could throw the ball all right. Stan could run. He was a good base runner. He didn't steal a lot of bases, but he didn't have to. He knew how to play. And he had good power."

Marion went on to say, "Tell you the kind of kid he was, I can remember when the '42 Series was over, Stan didn't come back to St. Louis to celebrate. He went from the New York station to Donora, and he was telling everybody goodbye, and he was crying like a baby."

Marion remembered his friend fondly: "I never saw Stan get mad with anybody. He was always kidding, a jovial person. He liked to tell jokes and play that damn harmonica. Stan's a very popular man."

After the 1943 season, Musial toured armed service camps in Alaska and the Aleutian Islands with Frankie Frisch, manager of the Pittsburgh Pirates, along with teammate Danny Litwhiler, Hank Borowy of the Yankees, and Dixie Walker of the Dodgers. Unfortunately, the weather was too cold to put on any demonstration games, although the players met with groups of men as often as possible, sometimes making up to six short jumps by plane a day. As for sports, they did take in one hockey game and got in some skiing. Musial later gave talks to the Lions and Rotary clubs in Donora, describing how he had spent Christmas Day in the cold north, where the nights were eighteen hours long and the wind and snow constant.

Before the start of the 1944 season, Musial tried to negotiate a new contract with Breadon, asking for a three-year deal totaling $40,000. Thanks to his .357 average and 347 total bases, Breadon did not have much room to negotiate but countered anyway with a $36,000 offer, which Musial accepted. The salary was scaled at $10,000, $12,500, and $13,500 for the third year, 1946.

Like many other Cardinals players, and particularly after his own experience negotiating for a raise after the 1943 season, Musial disliked Breadon, whom he regarded as a skinflint. Most of the players understandably thought they were underpaid in comparison with their National League peers. Breadon was even able to use the economy measures caused by the war to turn a profit. For one thing, the loss of regulars to the military meant a smaller payroll. The federal government had also imposed restrictions on raising salaries as a means of controlling inflation, which only gave Breadon further reason to chide players to be satisfied with their current pay. Even though attendance at Cardinals games sagged in 1942 and 1943, the Cardinals were still able to operate in the black because they were pennant contenders. As a result, the Cardinals posted an increase of $410,587 in profits during the war years.

On April 22, 1944, Musial was ordered by his draft board in Pennsylvania to report for his physical induction examination. The young slugger requested that the exam be transferred to Jefferson Barracks in St. Louis and quipped, "Well, I've just written a letter to my wife and now I'll add a little postscript to it." On May 16, at Jefferson Barracks, he underwent his physical and was accepted for navy service. At twenty-three, he faced a possible early call-up, but the following month, on June 23, the *Donora Herald-American* reported that their local hero would be with his team for at least another month, and perhaps longer. "It depends on how well we can fill our quotas," a local draft board clerk was quoted as saying. "We are calling single men ahead of the married registrants."

Musial avoided the draft in 1943 and 1944 only because the Selective Service board in Donora had enough available young men to exempt him temporarily. He was higher on the list because he was married with a son born before Pearl Harbor; in addition, he was the financial support of his parents. Lukasz's health had been deteriorating in recent years, especially after he suffered a stroke, and in 1943, though still in his early fifties, he retired from working in the zinc mines. Both to supplement his income and to stay in the good graces of the Selective Service System, Musial continued to work during the off-season in the zinc works—a war-related industry. There is no evidence that he sought special consideration from the draft board.

Throughout the war years, Musial still considered Donora his home, though he maintained an apartment in St. Louis not far from Sportsman's Park on Grand Avenue in the Fairgrounds Hotel. Lil and the Musials' first child, Dickie, often joined him. In St. Louis their social life revolved around other Cardinals players, notably the Marions, the Harry Walkers, and the Danny Litwhilers. Another close friend was local businessman Ed Carson and his wife, Sue, who were loyal baseball fans and had met Stan during his rookie year. Like the Musials, the Carsons had small children and modest tastes.

In the 1944 season, Musial and the high-flying Cardinals had stretched their lead to 10 ½ games by July 4. Three days later, Musial walloped his hundredth hit of the season, and on July 11 he appeared in the All-Star game at Forbes Field in Pittsburgh, playing both center field and right field. His only hit, a single, in four at bats drove in a run in the National League's first victory since 1940. In their march to the pennant, the Cardinals seemed indomitable. In mid-August they swept a four-game series with the Dodgers and equaled a National League record, set in 1907 by the Cubs, of winning their seventy-third contest in their first hundred games. They now held a whopping 18 ½ game lead over the rest of the league, and Southworth was rewarded with a two-year extension on his contract. It was the first time Breadon had ever extended a manager's pact. Since 1940, when Southworth signed on, the Cardinals had won 452 games while losing 220, for an extraordinary .673 percentage.

On August 18 the Cardinals won their eightieth game with a 5 to 0 victory over the New York Giants—the earliest date that a team had ever reached this milestone. They achieved that feat even though Musial was in a batting slump, which had brought down his average to .348. Walker Cooper, eight points ahead, had taken over as the team's leading slugger.

Musial's hopes of winning the batting title that year dimmed appreciably in September after he collided with Debs Garms as they raced into right center field chasing a fly ball hit by Cubs catcher Dewey Williams. Though Garms suffered bruises and cuts, Musial sustained a huge gash under his left eye and left the field on a stretcher. He was taken to a local hospital for X-rays. Though nothing was broken, he missed the next nine games and lost whatever chance he had to reach the 200-hit mark or to capture either the team batting title from Cooper or the National League title from Brooklyn's Dixie Walker. In Musial's absence, the Cardinals lost eight of those nine games, and fifteen out of their last twenty. But on the last day of the regular season, Musial seemed finally to return to form. In a doubleheader in New York against the Giants, he went 6 for 9.

The 1944 World Series was a rude awakening for Musial's wife, Lil. The Fairgrounds Hotel, where she and her husband lived during the summer, was literally within earshot of Sportsman's Park on Grand Avenue. Before the Series, the Browns and Cardinals not only swapped dugouts but hotel rooms, and on days when the Browns were playing at home, Lil often noticed how quiet the neighborhood was—in contrast to those days when the Cardinals were dressed in white.

But during the Browns' home-stretch playoffs against the Yankees in the last days of 1944, the stadium was "close to bedlam," Musial later recalled. "After the Series opener, Lil said, dazedly, 'This is a Brownie town.'"

That was not entirely true, of course. If anything, the fans were simply cheering for, and then celebrating, the all–St. Louis World Series. Win or lose, Stan Musial even then was the town's most popular and acclaimed sports hero in a decade. Not since the great Rogers Hornsby had locals ever seen the like.

War Games

Baseball was the number one morale booster among American servicemen during World War II, and it also helped keep the soldiers physically fit. By June 6, 1944, the day of the Normandy invasion, 1.5 million American servicemen were stationed in Britain alone, and along with letters and gift packages, U.S.O. clubs, and movies and radio programs, baseball was their lifeline back to America.

But baseball had a special importance, and servicemen played whenever and wherever they could. In Europe, pickup games amid the ruins of towns formerly occupied by the Nazis were commonplace. In fact, America's best baseball teams during World War II were probably not in the major leagues but in the army and the navy, according to William B. Mead in *Baseball Goes to War*.

Professional baseball paid a price for America's victory in the war. More than 500 major-league players ultimately swapped flannels for khakis, and such prominent players as Ted Williams, Joe DiMaggio, and Stan Musial all eventually served their nation in uniform.

After the United States declared war on December 8, 1941, professional ballplayers—though at first very few of the major players—either were drafted or enlisted by the thousands. The Selective Service Act of 1940 required that every able-bodied male between the ages of eighteen and sixty-five had to register, though initially the primary age bracket subject to the draft was between ages twenty-one and twenty-eight.

The Selective Service System (sss) operated according to a complicated code. The first men to be drafted were bachelors with no dependents. The next most eligible were single men with "collateral" dependents, such as parents, but without a job that contributed to the war effort. Next were single men with collateral dependents and a war-related job. Fourth came married men with no children and no war-related job, followed by married men without children but with a job that contributed to the war effort. Sixth in line were married men with children but no contributing job. Seventh and last were married men with children and a job that was war-related.

Further complicating the complicated code was the definition of what exactly distinguished a job that contributed to the war effort. In October 1942, sss headquarters issued a list of ninety-two jobs in the field of communications that qualified. These ranged from newspaper editor to telephone repairmen. Yet this list was only a recommendation, and local draft boards were free to decide for themselves which jobs were important and which were not. They could also decide whether a man with an important job could be replaced by a woman or by another man who was exempt from the draft. Standards varied from community to community, as did the number of men available to meet local draft quotas. Some local boards had no trouble meeting their quotas; others, particularly in rural areas, had a much harder time. As a result, a married man living in a large city had a much better chance of not being drafted than a married man living in the country.

Further, sss regulations did not specify that a twenty-one-year-old man was any more eligible than a forty-five-year-old man. Both, in the eyes of the draft code, were equally liable to be drafted. As a result, the army soon found itself encumbered with numerous older soldiers who could not survive the rigors of basic training. In September 1942 Senator Robert Taft, an influential Ohio Republican, called for the induction of men eighteen and nineteen years old "and accused President Roosevelt of planning to postpone such a move until after the congressional elections that November."

The following month, Roosevelt asked Congress to lower the draft age to eighteen. Henry L. Stimson, the secretary of war, announced that the administration's goal was an armed force of 7.5 million men by the end of 1943. At the time, the number stood at 4.25 million—too few, Stimson said, and "too old." Men in their late thirties and forties were to be discharged as they were replaced by eighteen- and nineteen-year-olds.

Although Congress appeared ready to approve the legislation calling for the induction of boys eighteen and nineteen, there was another major problem it had to contend with—one that aroused greater passions and was potentially far more politically divisive. Back in 1933 Prohibition had been repealed, but a coalition of temperance groups had been looking for an opportunity to reinstate the federal prohibition on the sale of alcoholic beverages. Now united into a formidable lobbying group known as the National Temperance and Prohibition Council were such groups as the Anti-Saloon League, the Women's Christian Temperance Union, the Methodist Board of Temperance, and the Prohibitionist Party, all active in pushing through the Volstead Act enacting Prohibition during World War I. The council, with a budget of $10 million, had a potent message for Congress: Who wanted innocent teenage soldiers exposed to the evils of alcohol?

When the bill to draft eighteen- and nineteen-year-olds reached the floor of Congress, Oklahoma Democrat Josh Lee put forward an amendment barring the sale of beer and liquor in the vicinity of military establishments. U.S. distilleries had already been ordered to make ethyl alcohol solely to be used by the military to help manufacture munitions—a fact which Lee and his supporters interpreted to mean that the United States had already officially declared the manufacture of drinking alcohol to be unnecessary. A report in the *New York Times* described the dry lobby as well organized and well financed, while the drinking majority was in disarray. At virtually the last moment, with the 1942 election only a week off, Senate leaders solved the problem by referring the amendment to a subcommittee for further study. On November 12 Congress voted to conscript eighteen- and nineteen-year-olds; those still in high school were allowed a six-month deferment to finish their studies, and agricultural workers were also deferred.

In early 1943 Manpower Commissioner Paul V. McNutt narrowed the grounds for deferment based on dependents, and listed twenty-nine occupations that were not war-related. These included dancing teacher, soda jerk, waiter, astrologer, and bartender; any man holding one of these jobs was now eligible for the draft, regardless of his family situation. Also newly eligible were men who worked in any of thirty-six nonessential businesses, including Turkish baths, florist shops, social-escort services—and baseball. Regarding the latter, McNutt explained, "The usefulness of the sport is a separate question from the 'essentiality' of individuals who play it. Thus it may well be that it is desirable that Blankville have a ball team. But Blankville may lose certain members of that team to higher priority industries—even members that might be 'essential' to winning the pennant. The pennant is not 'essential.'"

Other sports met with the same fate, with the singular exception of horse racing, since many jockeys were under eighteen. In boxing, 2,700 fighters were in service, including 31 past or present former champions.

Branch Rickey, among other baseball officials, agreed with McNutt's ruling, noting,

> If Bob Hope and Fred Allen and Jack Benny and others can do a better job carrying a rifle than they are doing right now, then, of course, essentiality compels them to change their jobs overnight. And if these 400 players now classed as 3-A [that is, with dependents] can do a better job for our 130 million people at anything other than playing this game this coming summer, then we want to know the way to do it and we are anxious to do it. By and large these men do not have any specialized skills in any other field of work, and neither women nor men past 38 can take over their present jobs. If there is a morale job to be done by baseball, these particular men must do it.

The reference to the movie industry was not incidental. On February 8, 1942, General Hershey had ruled, in response to a movie-industry petition for deferment of essential employees, that movie production was "an activity essential in certain instances to the national health, safety, and interest, and in other instances to war production." As a result, draft boards in California were directed to defer "actors, directors, writers, producers, cameramen, sound engineers, and other technicians" who could not be replaced. Hollywood entertainment was viewed as a prime propaganda tool to persuade the American public to support the war effort.

The uncertainty surrounding the eligibility of baseball players affected trades between the 1942 and 1943 seasons. "Would I like to trade?" asked Mel Ott, manager of the New York Giants. "Yes. But whom would I trade, and whom would the other clubs trade to me? And if I made a trade, how sure would I be that the man I got would report to me around March 1?"

A skit performed by the Circus Saints and Sinners, a social organization, at the Waldorf-Astoria Hotel in New York that winter illustrated baseball's predicament. In the skit, entitled "World Series of 1943," the character portraying Commissioner Landis ruled that no team could carry more than four players, and none could be physically able. "Four aged players hobbled onstage with the help of canes, crutches, and nurses administering vitamin hypodermics."

Perhaps the baseball man with the most illustrious military reputation was Larry MacPhail, general manager of the Brooklyn Dodgers, who in late 1942 gave up a $70,000 salary to accept a commission as an army lieutenant colonel. Back on January 6, 1919, shortly after the Armistice that ended World War I was declared, MacPhail and seven other soldiers had set out on an unauthorized mission to kidnap Kaiser Wilhelm, the leader of wartime Germany, who was then a refugee living at the castle of Count von Bentinck at Amerongen, Holland. Though MacPhail and his cohorts succeeded in disarming a guard and making their way into the kaiser's drawing room, they were frightened away by German soldiers. On his way out, MacPhail grabbed one of the kaiser's ashtrays as a souvenir.

In September 1942 J. G. Taylor Spink, the editor and publisher of the *Sporting News*, the "bible of baseball," wrote an editorial emblazoned with angelic wings and headlined "Look Well at These Heroes, for They Go." A rousing piece of patriotic purple prose that celebrated the "heroes of the diamond" both on the field and on the war front, the editorial concluded, "Look well at these heroes, for they go. . . . They go to fight and they go to come back. But if they don't return, theirs will be the Valhalla of Eddie Grant. . . . Look well at these heroes, for they go." Eddie Grant, the first major-league ballplayer killed in World War I, was increasingly being cited as an example of the baseball player as war hero. Judge Landis even suggested that he be elected to the Hall of Fame, "an honor that would have been based on his death rather than his lifetime batting average of .249."

Another World War I–era player to enjoy a revival was Hank Gowdy, the first player to enlist in that war. Matching Spinks in lofty patriotic sentiment, Gowdy, now coaching for the Cincinnati Reds, told the *Sporting News*, "I have been the recipient of many honors in my lengthy baseball career, and also have been in receipt of honors outside the realm of baseball. But the highest honor of my entire life came through being privileged to wear the United States Army uniform and serve my country in the last war in which it was engaged." Leaving no doubt that he meant what he said, Gowdy enlisted, in early 1943, at age fifty-three, and was commissioned as an army captain.

Stripped of almost three-fourths of its manpower, organized baseball turned to older men and even retirees, as well as those that the Selective Service boards had classified as 4-F, or unfit for service, for physical, mental, or moral reasons. Even a few teenagers—some under the age of eighteen—were recruited to play ball. On the other hand, numerous minor-league franchises had to shut down soon after America went to war, owing to a lack of players and funds.

Yet baseball seemed to prosper as never before on other fronts, far from the familiar stadiums and ballparks in big cities and small towns across the United States. Every branch of service, whether army, navy, or marines, set up competitive leagues and played games, if possible, with nearby major-league teams. One such service team, at the Norfolk Naval Training Station in Virginia, was "so loaded with past, present, and future professional players talent that they competed successfully with most major-league baseball teams they faced." The military also established teams and leagues as an indispensable morale booster at bases in Europe and the Pacific.

The popularity of baseball during the war may also be attributable to the fact that 1941, the last year of peacetime, was one of the most glorious in the sport's history. Robert Creamer, in *Baseball in '41*, has called it "the greatest baseball season that ever was." That was the year "Joltin' Joe" DiMaggio hit safely in a record fifty-six straight games, and when the Boston Red Sox's Ted Williams finished the season with a .406 batting average, a feat that to this day has not been equaled. Not to be outdone, the Brooklyn Dodgers, like the Browns a perennial cellar dweller, hired a new manager, Leo Durocher, and saw their fortunes dramatically change as they won the National League pennant.

Early in 1941 there was considerable speculation about who would be the first major-league baseball star to be drafted, and the consensus was that it would be Hank Greenberg, the premier slugger for the Detroit Tigers, since his draft number was 621. The *Sporting News* called him "Baseball's Good Soldier." But the team asked a local draft board to grant Greenberg a deferment, and he was given a brief reprieve. As it turned out, the first professional ballplayer to be drafted was Hugh "Losing Pitcher" Mulcahy, who played with the Philadelphia Phillies and was drafted in early March 1941. Two months later, Greenberg was told to report to an antitank company in Fort Custer, Michigan. Immediately, his salary plunged from $55,000 a year to $21 a month.

Uncomplaining, Greenberg told the *Sporting News*, "I have made a lot of money in a short time in baseball, and I leave well situated financially. I've been lucky enough also to make some good investments. Taxes being what they are, I'm not crying." He was immediately assigned to the Second Division baseball team. In November, with America still not at war and Greenberg on the eve of his thirty-first birthday, he was released. Before the year was out, though, he would be back in khaki. Such uncertainty was paradigmatic of the difficulties American society was adjusting to at the time.

DiMaggio and Williams, however, were the two most conspicuous examples of major-league ballplayers who were in no hurry to exchange a baseball for a service uniform. The army in particular had a tacit policy of trying to be as lenient as possible with athletes. Golfer Porky Oliver was given a four-day leave to compete in a tournament, while Bummy David received a month's leave to train for a fight with Fritzie Zivic for the welterweight boxing championship. This was the army's way of showing its "human side," an attitude supported by the American public. A 1941 Gallup poll asked whether big-league ballplayers should be exempted from the draft until the baseball season was over, and 84 percent answered "yes." But when the Japanese attacked Pearl Harbor on December 7, 1941, all such questions became moot. So many men were volunteering for the draft that one of the problems major-league baseball faced was whether to cancel the 1942 season; and if not, to figure out how to replace those players who were certain to be drafted in the war years to come.

Some baseball owners advocated more night games. One baseball executive decidedly opposed to that radical novelty was the Dodgers' ever-thrifty Branch Rickey, who worried that night baseball might become so popular it would take the place of daytime ball. "You don't have to pay for sunshine," he pointed out. He was seconded by Babe Ruth, who had hit all 714 of his home runs in daylight. The Sultan of Swat warned that night games would not only ruin players' eyes but deprive them of sleep, while the dampness might make them liable to colds. He might have added that night games would also interfere with their carousing—a subject on which he was baseball's foremost expert.

At their annual meeting in Chicago on January 8, 1942, the owners of professional baseball teams voted to provide funds to give equipment to the men in service, and to donate $100,000 from the next All-Star game to the fund as well. That same month, 18,000 baseballs and 4,500 Louisville Sluggers and other professional-quality bats were sent to camps in the United States. On January 15, 1942, President Franklin Delano Roosevelt gave Major League Baseball the green light to proceed with the upcoming season. Judge Landis had written to him a day earlier, asking whether organized baseball should close for the duration of the war or remain open. Roosevelt replied:

> I honestly feel that it would be best for the country to keep baseball going. There will be fewer people unemployed and everybody will work longer hours and harder than ever before.

And that means that they ought to have a chance for recreation and for taking their minds off their work even more than before.

Baseball provides a recreation that does not last over two hours or two hours and a half and which can be got for very little cost. And, incidentally, I hope that night games can be extended because it gives an opportunity for the day shift to see a game occasionally.

As to the players themselves I know you agree with me that individual players who are of active military or naval age should go, without question, into the services. Even if the actual quality of the teams is lowered by the greater use of older players, this will not dampen the popularity of the sport. . . .

Here is another way of looking at it—if 300 teams use 5,000 or 6,000 players, these players are a definite recreational asset to at least 20,000,000 of their fellow citizens—and that in my judgment is thoroughly worthwhile.

By the end of 1941, 300 players had already gone into service. Hank Greenberg, only recently discharged from the army, patriotically signed up again after Pearl Harbor, explaining to the *Sporting News*, "We are in trouble, and there is only one thing for me to do—return to service. I have not been called back. I am going back of my own accord. This doubtless means I am finished with baseball, and it would be silly to say I do not leave it without a pang. But all of us are confronted with a terrible task—the defense of our country and the fight for our lives."

Greenberg was followed into the service by Cleveland Indians star pitcher Bob Feller, who was sworn in by former boxing champion Gene Tunney, now a lieutenant commander in the navy. The induction was broadcast on the radio, and afterward Feller told the listening audience, "There are many things more important than baseball these days. First we'll have to win the war to keep baseball."

Ted Williams, on the day Pearl Harbor was bombed, was out duck hunting in Princeton, Minnesota, and heard the news while eating breakfast in his hotel room. He had been classified 3-A because he was the sole support of his mother, but by January was reclassified 1-A. During this period he "endured constant criticism from members of the press as well as fans for not enlisting in the service." Matters only got worse when he reported for spring training and his draft status was briefly changed to 2-A; then he was put back into 3-A. The press criticized Williams not because reporters thought he was trying to get out of service but because he had not rushed to enlist as Greenberg had. The coverage in the newspapers and on radio was so negative that Quaker Oats canceled its $4,000 endorsement contract with the Red Sox's star. Finally, in May 1942 Williams signed up for the navy's aviation division. While learning to fly the F4U at a base in Jacksonville, Florida, eagle-eyed Williams set a new student gunnery record.

"If I can make a success of flying," Williams later nonchalantly told a reporter, "I'd just as soon stay in service—provided I could get a month off once in a while to go hunting."

Clearly, he missed duck hunting more than baseball.

Joe DiMaggio also received public criticism for not signing up quickly enough. Typical was a letter from M. M. Caretti of New York to the sports editor of the *New York Times* published on January 31, 1942. "Men have been drafted into the Army who never have earned more than a small salary in civilian life, who had no sideline returns to fall back on, and who had wives and children to support," said Caretti. "On the other hand, especially in baseball, there are quite a few, too many, who have been exempted from service. A case in point is Joe DiMaggio of the Yankees. Why he ever was exempted from service is beyond comprehension. Not that he is the only one, however. It seems to me that men well known in sport should take the lead in volunteering for their country in time of need and not wait to be drafted, much less accept exemption."

Public speculation was that DiMaggio's military status was mixed up with his marital difficulties. DiMaggio was married to Dorothy Arnold, who before her marriage to Joltin' Joe had been a movie actress. In December 1942 she went to Reno to seek a divorce. The DiMaggios also had a baby, which meant that if the couple remained together, DiMaggio could obtain an exemption as a father. The *Sporting News* reported that Yankee president Ed Barrow might act as a marriage counselor. For a time, the DiMaggios were able to resolve their difficulties, and DiMaggio, age twenty-eight, was given a 3-A draft classification. But then, in February 1943, without bothering to notify the Yankee organization, he joined the army. Perhaps he did not bother to tell the team of his plans because they had sent him a 1943 contract that called for a pay cut from $43,750 to $40,000. He also refused the furlough soldiers were allowed to take before beginning their service.

In January 1943 Commissioner Landis ordered all sixteen major-league baseball teams to conduct their spring training north of the Mason-Dixon line. He was responding to a request from Joseph B. Eastman, director of the Office of Defense Transportation, not to tax the nation's railroads with unnecessary travel during wartime. Similarly, Eastman suggested less travel for preseason exhibition games. Accordingly, Landis promised Eastman that all the teams would train in the north and revise their playing schedules so that each team would visit its seven competitors only three times during the regular season instead of four. The major leagues grandly calculated that, as a result of the cutbacks and considering the number of players, coaches, sportswriters, and others involved, they were reducing their travel requirements in 1943 by five million "man miles."

Midwestern teams had the advantage in securing new sites for spring training, since few colleges on the Atlantic seaboard had field houses while they were plentiful in the Midwest—in Indiana, in particular. The Chicago White Sox and Chicago Cubs found a new home in the hot springs resort community of French Lick, while the Cincinnati Reds settled in at Indiana University in Bloomington. The Cleveland Indians were welcomed at Purdue University in Lafayette, the Minneapolis Millers of the American Association at Terre Haute, the Detroit Tigers at Evansville, and the Pittsburgh Pirates at Muncie.

In the East, the Boston Braves chose Choate, the exclusive boys' prep school in Wallingford, Connecticut. The Red Sox trained at Tufts College in Medford, Massachusetts; the Brooklyn Dodgers at Bear Mountain, New York; the New York Giants at Lakewood, New Jersey; the Yankees at Asbury Park, New Jersey; the Philadelphia Athletics in Wilmington, Delaware; the Phillies in Hershey, Pennsylvania; and the Washington Senators at the University of Maryland in College Park, where they slept in fraternity houses.

Landis had effectively ruled out training camps south of the Ohio or Potomac rivers, but the two St. Louis teams were allowed more southerly sites as long as they were not too far from home. The fact that there was a gambling casino near both Cairo and Cape Girardeau—just north of Cairo, on the Illinois side of the Mississippi—was an added attraction for the players.

On one particularly wintry day at the Giants camp, a group of navy men decided to play a practical joke on the players by dropping a few baseballs from a blimp 400 feet in the air. Both first baseman Phil Weintraub and outfielder Danny Gardella managed to make a catch. Not to be outdone in the antics department, the Athletics once took sleighs to an indoor workout at their camp. At the Cubs facility, the players once did their calisthenics indoors to the piano accompaniment of manager Charlie Grimes.

The weather that spring turned out to be unusually miserable. Cardinals trainer Harrison J. Weaver ordered long underwear for all the players. In French Lick, the White Sox found their field under four feet of muddy water, while the Cubs' field, laid out on a golf course, was under three feet. The Cardinals and Browns, along with the Red Sox and Indians, had the good fortune of having indoor training facilities for bad weather, while the Dodgers were permitted to use the field house of the nearby U.S. Military Academy at West Point, but only when it was not being used by army cadets. Not infrequently, Brooklyn players were summoned to use the field house at night or early in the morning, and occasionally they had to interrupt their drills when the field was abruptly preempted by academy officials.

Billy Southworth, manager of the Cardinals, took a sanguine view of the situation, telling a reporter, "That occasional indoor drill is a good break, rather than an interruption in our routine. You see, the early outdoor work makes the muscles sore and the indoor work warms them up and takes out the soreness. I believe we have hit upon an excellent way of getting into condition."

Joe McCarthy, the Yankee manager, offered a more cynical perspective, complaining, "I am not training a basketball team or a track squad. . . . I am dead set against training indoors," noting that some players might strain their eyes in artificial light or get too accustomed to wearing sneakers instead of spiked shoes—or, worse, forget how to throw against the wind.

Another "hardship" baseball players had to get used to was mixing with common soldiers on the trains. In the past, they had always enjoyed private cars and lower berths. Now they had to make do with upper berths, or ride on a day coach if an overnight trip was not required.

Baseball was affected in less noticeable ways as well. "Cracker Jacks, a ballpark staple in fact as well as in song, had to give up prizes made in Japan and turn to domestic substitutes." Virtually everything was rationed: tires, cars, sugar, gasoline, bicycles, men's work shoes and rubber boots, fuel oil, coffee, processed foods, stoves, meats, and fats. A man's suit could not be made with pleats, a vest, or a second pair of trousers. In Detroit, automobile manufacturers stopped making new models after 1942. In October 1941 General Motors ran this advertisement: "We resolved on a 1942 automobile of such merit as would carry the Buick reputation without fault until other new Buicks, however far off, would come along and refresh it. . . . It would be a shame, for you and for us, to have you miss the dreadnought Buick we've built to stand up successfully to the toughest job in years."

Traveling baseball teams were frequently served meatless dinners. Responding to their husbands' yearning for beef and as a spur to getting a slimmer figure, the wives of four Philadelphia Phillies players dieted to save ration points so they could purchase extra meat when their husbands played at home.

But alarms went off when wartime restrictions struck at the very heart of baseball—the ball itself. Before the war, baseballs were covered with horsehide imported from Belgium and rural France, where young horses were slaughtered for their meat. After the German occupation of those countries, horsehide was imported from Bolivia until the supply ran out in 1943. A domestic grade of horsehide was then substituted, though more than a dozen tanning formulas had to be tested before one passed muster.

Cork, used to make the core of the ball, was also no longer available. Two different alternative baseball cores now had to be considered. After the government banned the wartime production of golf balls, thousands of golf ball cores had been orphaned, and the National League wanted to use these as a substitute. The American League, though, preferred to use a core made of granulated cork, a plentiful variety, with a double shell of balata, a hard rubberlike material used to make the covers of golf balls. After comparative testing, the "balata ball" was chosen. Commissioner Landis ordered the A. G. Spalding Co. to make the ball as resilient as the ball used in 1939, because since that year batting averages had been steadily declining, and, noted William B. Mead in *Baseball Goes to War*, "the fans were thought to prefer a lustier game." Instead, the new ball turned out to be "as dead as a rock."

In the first eleven major-league games in which the balata ball was used, no home runs were hit; and of the first twenty-nine games of the season, eleven were shutouts. Stan Musial was an exception, hitting a blue streak, yet many of his best drives were being caught short of the fences. Only then did he realize, he said, "the plight of old-time players who complained of the dead ball that was used in the major leagues before Babe Ruth glamorized the home run."

Spalding defended the new ball, to no avail. The *New York Daily News* asked the Cooper Union Institute of Technology to test the new ball, and the institute reported that the balata ball was 25.9 percent less resilient than the 1942 baseball. Warren Giles, general manager of the Cincinnati Reds, threatened to import an outlaw ball made especially for his team. Reluctantly, Spalding acknowledged that its own tests had also shown that the balata ball was defective, primarily because of a wartime "rubber" cement made of reprocessed rubber—Japanese military forces now controlled most of the world's rubber plantations. Balls made with a better grade of cement were then rushed into production; in the meantime, baseballs left over from 1942 were used. Finally, in the winter of 1943, the War Production Board allowed Spalding to use cork and synthetic rubber, and the company tried to put the painful memory of the balata ball behind it. The gratifying result, for both players and fans, was a total of 10,353 runs scored in 1944, compared to 9,704 the previous season.

In the eastern United States, German submarines were sinking oil tankers sailing between the Gulf Coast and New York and other eastern ports, which soon led to an oil shortage. On February 8, 1942, U-boats sank the Socony-Vacuum Oil Company's *China Arrow* a hundred miles off the New York coast, the fourteenth such vessel to be sunk in less than a month. Another six had been sunk off Canada. Railroads and trucks were able to carry only half as much oil from the southwestern oil fields to the East Coast as was needed. Gasoline rationing was imposed in seventeen eastern states in early 1942, while families and businesses were urged to keep their thermostats down to sixty-eight degrees. Times Square also went dark for the first time since 1917. Both the Polo Grounds and Ebbets Field, the respective homes of the Giants and Dodgers, were allowed only one hour of artificial light. "Army officials decided that the glare would invite trouble at sea," the *Sporting News* reported, "and perhaps guide some suicide flier bearing a grim message from Dizzy Adolf, and ordered the two ballparks blacked out." Similarly, since many of the tankers were sunk at night, military authorities feared they might be silhouetted by the bright lights on shore and thus be easy targets for U-boats. Coastal communities were ordered to dim their lights in the evenings.

Baseball's solution to the dimouts was the "twi-night" game, an innovation originally advanced only by the Giants and Dodgers. Yankee Stadium had no lights, and night games in inland cities were not thought to pose a risk. Yet twi-night games, also called "dusk" games, soon caught on in other cities as well, though they were banned on the Pacific Coast. Umpires also helped to speed up the game by not allowing infielders to throw the ball around after an out.

The war caused particular problems for minor-league baseball. In 1943 twenty-three leagues folded. The problem was not just how to supply the minors with players during wartime, but how to anticipate the future of the system when an overwhelming number of players would be returning after the end of the war. One visionary with a suggestion was Clarence Rowland, president of the Los Angeles Angels and soon to be head of the Pacific Coast League. Rowland's solution was to persuade his fellow PCL owners to form a third major league. Yet the idea was not really feasible. Although the PCL was the premier minor-league circuit in the country, its parks were not on a par with major-league stadiums either in quality or in size. With the exception of the Angels, attendance was also far below that of most major-league teams.

Several baseball owners put forth plans of their own to solve the problem of what to do with the minor leagues and how to anticipate the postwar return of ballplayers. Clark Griffith, owner of the Washington Senators, suggested that major-league teams be allowed to own only three minor-league teams. That way they would not be able to stockpile the best players—certainly a primary concern of the lowly Senators. Jack Zoller, general manager of the Detroit Tigers, proposed a controversial plan to allow minor-league teams to scout and develop players, while permitting each major-league team to control only fifty players. "The majors would then have to purchase the players from the minor league team when a player was ready to be promoted."

The Dodgers' Branch Rickey would have nothing to do with these schemes and wanted to maintain the status quo. "It is utopian," he sneered, vis-à-vis Zoller's plan. "He has the wrong approach to the entire question and [the plan] does not interest me." As events proved, neither Zoller's nor Griffith's plan came to fruition. After the war, with the return of thousands of players, the minor leagues boomed as never before, expanding back up to forty-one leagues.

Another controversy facing baseball during the war years was whether to allow ballplayers to work in war plants. With more manpower needed for the war effort, the Selective Service System had eventually reduced its classifications, for all practical purposes, to just two: 1-A for men eligible to go into service, and 4-F for those unqualified to serve. The majority of professional baseball players during the war were classified either 4-F or were older than thirty-eight, which made them automatically ineligible.

The Browns and the Philadelphia Athletics led the majors in lobbying for permission to use on weekends those players who worked in war plants. These men made up the only other significant draft classification, 2-B, or men who were physically eligible for the draft but were deferred because they worked in a war-related effort. If they played full-time, of course, they would be eligible for the draft. Again, Rickey, along with the Yankees' Ed Barrow, opposed using these players, but Commissioner Landis gave permission anyway. As a result, players such as Frank Crosetti, Denny Galehouse, and Chet Laabs, all of whom worked in war plants, were permitted to play.

Yet another problem baseball owners had to solve was how to compensate returning players. At their annual winter meeting in 1943, they came up with a plan that would give players their salaries at the level they were at when they entered the armed services. They were also to be allowed a "fair" chance of making the parent team; if they did not make the club, they would be sent to the minors at a level at least one classification above the one they were obtained at.

The 1944 season saw the signing of several very young players in an attempt to fill the roster. On June 10, 1944, a fifteen-year-old named Joe Nuxhall became the youngest player in major-league history when he stepped onto the mound for the Cincinnati Reds in a game against the Cardinals. The Reds were already trailing, 13 to 0, and obviously thought they had nothing to lose in seeing how Nuxhall might perform. He only made matters worse, giving up five runs on two hits and five walks in two-thirds of an inning. On a happier note, Nuxhall returned to baseball in 1952 and wound up winning 135 major-league games.

Somewhat more successful than Nuxhall was Tommy Brown, a sixteen-year-old high schooler who made his debut for the Dodgers on August 3, when he hit a double and scored a run. Brown went on to play for nine seasons, compiling a batting average of .241. A minor-league teenage sensation was seventeen-year-old Mario Picone, who played for Bristol, a New York Giants team in the Appalachian League. On June 15 Picone struck out twenty-eight batters in a nineteen-inning game against Johnson City. As a professional, though, Picone appeared in only thirteen games over three seasons with the Giants and Reds between 1947 and 1954.

In 1944, with the Cardinals, Browns, and other teams battling for the pennant, sports news understandably took a back seat to the momentous events in the Pacific and in Europe—the Allies' capture of Rome, D-day, Germany's launch of v-1 flying bombs against Britain, the Battle of the Philippines, the unsuccessful Rastenburg plot by German military officers to assassinate Hitler, the liberation of Paris in late August.

All baseball games were canceled on June 6 when the Allied forces landed on the beaches of Normandy, and Americans were urged to pray for the success of the invasion. Several professional ballplayers were among those who would perform valiantly on D-day. Among them was former Dodger Larry French, who later recalled, "The beach was plenty hot, 88 mm. fire, mines wherever you stepped, and the darndest fireworks each night you can imagine." Minor-league pitcher John Pinder was killed while heroically rescuing radio equipment from his boat, stranded a hundred yards from shore. The equipment allowed the Allies to establish radio contact on the beaches to set up air and sea support. "The first time he went into the water to get the equipment, shrapnel hit him. As he went back into the water, which was engulfed in flames, he was shot in the head and was holding the left side of his face in his hand as he got more of the radio tools. After he set up the radio, he went back to get more equipment, and was blasted by more machine gun fire, yet continued to refuse treatment. John went on until he eventually was weakened and died."

During the mighty contest between the Browns and Cardinals, another "World Series" was being played in the Pacific war theater between the army and navy teams. The rules of the game dictated that, as in professional baseball, the title go to the winner in a best-of-seven matchup. Later the rule was changed to best of nine, with all games to be played even if the title was already locked up, since they had proved to be so popular. The early games were held in Oahu, and later ones in Maui and the Valley Isle. The navy handily won the first six games, with the army getting its two victories only after the schedule was extended to nine games. The ninth game was tied 4 to 4 in the eighth inning when Tom Ferrick, a former pitcher for the Cleveland Indians, aided his own cause by singling in left fielder Schoolboy Rowe, also a former major-league pitcher, and put his team in front. Phil Rizzuto, the former New York Yankee, then squeezed Pee-Wee Reese across the plate with another run, and navy won the contest 6 to 4, and the Armed Forces World Series 7 games to 2.

Just before the start of the Series, baseball officials announced that five troupes of major leaguers from both the National and American leagues would head overseas soon after the fall classic was completed to entertain soldiers in frontline battle areas under the auspices of the U.S.O. camp shows. The volunteers who signed up for the tours, each of which was to last two to three months, included eleven active players and six managers, as well as several former players, two umpires, and five sportswriters. Luke Sewell was one of the managers who had enlisted, along with Mel Ott of the New York Giants, Leo Durocher of the Dodgers, and Frankie Frisch of the Pirates. Players included Don Gutteridge of the Browns, Dutch Leonard of the Senators, and Nick Etten, Johnny Lindell, and Tuck Stainback of the Yankees.

In the end, World War II inadvertently produced one of the most fabulous pennant races in baseball history, saw the inauguration of the farm system and a struggle for the future of minor-league baseball, and also of necessity welcomed very young teenagers into the game, many of whom were to make their mark in a way never seen before or since. In addition, baseball was the first public arena in the struggle for integration. Many of the enlisted mens' leagues in the military were interracial. In this way, World War II laid the groundwork for the later use of both black and Latino players in major-league ball. For a time, even women were admitted, with the establishment of the All-American Girls Professional Baseball League. The use of women and minorities in professional baseball more than in any other sport not only revolutionized professional sports and amateur athletics but anticipated the civil rights movement of the 1960s.

Lightning in a Bottle

In game 3 the St. Louis Browns bounced back "with the resilience of a pre-war rubber ball," John Drebinger reported in the *New York Times*. In doing so, they "once more tossed baseball's outstanding academic minds into complete consternation," thrashing the supposedly infinitely superior Cardinals to move back into the lead.

This time, the win was no fluke. Perhaps psychologically the Browns were feeling more at home, since they were now suited up in their faded white home uniforms for the first time. The two teams had traded not only dugouts but also, it seemed, a winning attitude. In their last home stays during the regular season, the Browns had won two out of three against the White Sox, two out of three against the Senators, three straight against the Athletics, two out of three against the Red Sox, and four straight from the Yankees.

"Things ought to perk up for us today," Sewell had drawled, emphasizing the point, as the Cardinals were unceremoniously shuttled over to the visitors' dugout on the first base line, "because we now have those guys on our own home field."

Even the program took note of the new situation. When the original program was sent to the printers, the editors did not know whether the Cardinals would be playing the Browns or the Tigers, so they compromised by announcing that the Series was to be "National League vs. American League." For game 3 the new cover boldly proclaimed: "Browns vs. Cardinals."

Even a few Cardinals seem to feel the spotlight had shifted. When a photographer approached Blix Donnelly, the star of game 2, and asked him to pose for a picture, Donnelly looked around, pointed to himself, and innocently asked, "Who, me?"

Just before the game was to begin, umpire Tom Dunn discerned an interloper on the playing field. A sailor had curled himself up inside the huge tarpaulin roll near the left field bullpen. Dunn gave him the thumb, and the serviceman reluctantly climbed back into the stands.

Unlike the two previous days, when overnight rain had given way to bright afternoon sunshine, this day was swelteringly hot, with temperatures well into the nineties. That did not prevent a record 34,737 fans from crowding into creaking Sportsman's Park.

In New York City, meanwhile, the nation was also observing another momentous ritual. Al Smith, the beloved governor of New York State, was to be buried that day from St. Patrick's Cathedral. At one o'clock that morning the Cathedral doors had finally been closed after the long line of mourners had diminished to a sprinkling.

For the showdown Billy Southworth and Luke Sewell had both decided to go with their seventeen-game winners, Ted Wilks and Jack Kramer, respectively. Wilks, a burly rookie control pitcher, had led the National League in winning percentage, with an .810 mark. Right-hander Kramer, a tall New Orleans native back from an eighteen-month hitch with the Seabees, was known for his winning streaks, and also for his losing streaks. At the start of the season he had won five in a row, then saw his record drop to below .500, and then had wound up the year by winning his last four decisions.

"Gosh, but it's hot," Kramer remarked as he picked up his glove and headed out for the mound. "And, brother, I don't like it when it's hot. But if the boys will just get a few hits and a few runs for me I should do all right."

Sewell decided to sit Chet Laabs, the hero of the final regular-season game against the Yankees, and replace him with Al Zarilla. In the first two contests, the luckless Laabs had gone 0 for 8, with five strikeouts.

Southworth also reinstalled Danny Litwhiler into the lineup and batted him leadoff. Hailing from Ringtown, Pennsylvania, the Dutchman, as he was affectionately known, had not batted number one since he came into the league with the Philadelphia Phillies in 1940. In this game, the experiment turned out to be less than successful, and he was easily dispatched by Kramer when he led off the first inning by soaring a fly ball to Zarilla in left field. Kramer then seemed well on his way to retiring Johnny Hopp, who hit a grounder to the shortstop Vern Stephens. But Stephens booted the ball, and suddenly Hopp, the "Nebraska Grasshopper," had hopped all the way to second. Musial then popped up to shallow left field for the second out, but Walker Cooper punched a long single just out of Stephens's reach to drive Hopp home. With a man on first and two out, the Cardinals had suddenly taken a quick 1 to 0 lead. Kramer then walked Ray Sanders. Up next was Whitey Kurowski, who took three straight balls, and Sewell signaled for Al Hollingsworth to start warming up in the bullpen. But Kramer finally settled down, and avoided loading up the bases by fanning Kurowski on three pitches.

"With reckless abandon," Drebinger sniffed in the *Times*, the Browns had "tossed a run to the Cards with an error in the first inning." But soon enough they would spring to life, and that little slip would be forgotten. Even the *Sporting News* allowed its prejudice to show, calling the moment Hopp crossed the plate "a tainted run."

In the second inning, the Browns had a scoring opportunity that went nowhere. Uncharacteristically, Wilks threw just one strike in walking the first two batters, Stephens and McQuinn. He then got Zarilla to fly out, while Christman hit into a fielder's choice. After walking Red Hayworth to load the bases, Wilks struck out Kramer to end the inning.

The Cardinals failed to produce another run in the top half of the third. But when the Browns came up to bat, their hometown rivals "caught lightning in a bottle," as Bob Broeg reported in *Leatherneck*. Broeg was quoting Leo Durocher, the garrulous manager of the Brooklyn Dodgers, from back during the 1941 World Series, when Brooklyn's "beloved bums" seemed about to even the crosstown classic against the world champion Yankees at two games each. In the last of the ninth inning, leading 4 to 3, Dodgers pitcher Hugh Casey quickly retired the first two batters. But then, within only one out of victory, he threw a third strike that not only fooled Tommy Henrich, who swung blindly and missed, but also his own catcher, Mickey Owen. The ball squirted out of Owen's glove, Henrich safely dashed to first, and the Yankees, "pardoned at the 11th hour," went on to collect four runs and win the game. Dispirited, the Dodgers lost the game on the following day as well. Brooklyn, as Durocher mumbled unbelievingly, "had caught lightning in a bottle."

In the third inning of game 3, the Cardinals managed to replicate the Dodgers' feat. Wilks started the bottom of the inning by retiring the first two batters. The Browns were showing little fire power at bat, and even hits by Moore and Stephens did not seem particularly threatening. Southworth was so unconcerned that he did not bother to signal to his bullpen to warm up. The Cardinals, after all, were still ahead, 1 to 0.

That third out never came. McQuinn, the next batter up, sliced a single to center, scoring Moore and tying the game. Then Zarilla banged his first hit, a line drive to left center field, which brought Stephens home and put the Browns ahead. Christman then belted a clothesline single over third base, and suddenly the score was 3 to 1 and the crowd was roaring. Head down, Wilks "walked the last mile to the showers," Broeg wrote, and big Fred "Fritz" Schmidt, who had warmed up too hurriedly too late, took over and fired off a wild pitch that bounced in front of the plate. Cooper tried to stop the ball, but it caromed off his glove, allowing Zarilla to sprint home, and when the dust cleared the mighty Cardinals were behind by the astounding score of 4 to 1. Those five straight hits with two men out were the "lightning in a bottle" that were to doom the Cardinals. The Browns' display of firepower in this inning was to be their best in the Series. Schmidt was then able to get Kramer to ground out to end the inning.

Kramer returned the favor, though, by retiring the Cardinals in order for the next three innings, striking out four in the process. Then, in the seventh, the Cardinals opened with a single to center by Sanders. As in the first inning, Kramer was to pay for the Browns' poor fielding. Kurowski, the next batter up, forced Sanders at second, but Gutteridge threw away the double-play relay to first, allowing Kurowski to reach second base. Marion then drove him home with a single to center.

But the Browns stormed back, scoring two more runs in their half of the inning off new pitcher Al Jurisch. Gutteridge, after eleven futile times at bat, finally whistled a double into right field. Kreevich then popped up to Marion, and Moore grounded to Sanders, while Gutteridge took third. Gutteridge then scored on a wild pitch to Stephens. McQuinn brought Stephens in when he rolled a long double down the right field foul line and Musial had trouble picking up the ball. All of the Browns runs in the game so far had been scored when there were two men out.

In the eighth inning, Sewell came out to check on Kramer's condition after Hopp singled and Walker Cooper doubled, sending Hopp to third. Hayworth assured the manager that his pitcher was fine. Taking his catcher's advice, Sewell let "Handsome Jack" stay in the game, and he responded to Sewell's vote of confidence by striking out Sanders and getting Kurowski to fly out. The rest of the game was anticlimactic. Kramer cruised through the ninth and the Browns won the game 6 to 2. Even though the Cardinals had turned in another near-flawless fielding day, they now trailed in the Series. Many Browns fans and sportswriters were murmuring that the Browns could have had a commanding 3 to 0 lead if not for Potter's double error in game 2, which took that contest into fatal extra innings.

After the game George Sisler, the Browns' former All-Star and Hall of Famer, was still reluctant to say outright whether he thought his old team would take the Series. He merely volunteered to Broeg that the Browns stood "a good chance" to win the championship.

"This is easily the most astonishing ball club ever to reach the Series," Daley concluded in the *Times*. "The Cardinals are a pre-war team of acknowledged strength and class. The Brownies are an ill-assorted collection of cast-offs. However, in three games the mighty Redbirds have made the startling total of two earned runs. Maybe it doesn't make sense, but that's the way this dizzy Series is going."

It was revealed after the game that Ted Wilks had spent the opening day of the Series in a local hospital for treatment of stomach ulcers.

Now that the Cardinals had lost game 3, they had tradition working against them. Since 1925 only one club, Cincinnati, had come back to win the Series after losing two of the first three games. The Reds turned that trick in 1940 at the expense of the Detroit Tigers.

Midnight Strikes

And then it was all over. The mighty Cardinals, like a slumbering giant, awoke from their bad dream and sent the Browns back to the lower depths of the American League and baseball oblivion.

Game 4 started on a somber note. Just before game time the crowd grew silent as a stocky, one-armed marine walked to the third-base line. The band, which had assembled at home plate, struck up "The Marine Hymn" as Cpl. Johnny Spillane stood at attention, his empty right sleeve hanging at his side. Many in the crowd had read Spillane's story that morning in the newspapers. Back in August 1941, he had turned down a contract to play for the St. Louis Cardinals to enlist in the Marine Corps. Sent to the Pacific, he had been in fierce combat with Japanese forces on the bloody beaches of Tarawa. At one point, he and the enemy had engaged in a duel of sorts, hurling hand grenades at each other, until one thrown by the Japanese landed at his feet before he could toss it back. The grenade exploded, and Spillane lost his arm. He was later awarded the Navy Cross, the Purple Heart, and two presidential citations.

Just before the start of the World Series, Spillane, a native of Waterbury, Connecticut, was recuperating in a naval hospital in Philadelphia when word got around that he wished he could see the Browns and the Cardinals compete for the world championship—a Series he might very well have played in but for the war. George Skouras, a wealthy theater magnate, heard about Spillane's predicament and arranged for him to arrive in St. Louis by the start of game 4. Spillane attended the game as a guest of Don Barnes, sitting with the Browns' owner in his box seat and rooting not for the Cardinals, who had once wanted to sign him up, but for the underdogs who had somehow managed to be leading the Series 2 to 1.

Before the game the Browns management announced a new policy.

Instead of asking fans to toss back all balls hit into the stands, to be sent to service teams, it encouraged them to keep the balls as souvenirs of the Series. The Browns promised to keep an exact count of "lost" balls and send an equivalent number to the services.

Sewell chose Sig Jakucki as his pitcher for the fourth game. But as Bob Broeg told his marine readers in *Leatherneck*, the contest was all but over by the twelfth pitch of the first inning. Short, wiry Harry "The Cat" Brecheen of the Cardinals turned out to be the dominating pitcher, despite "his limited tools of the pitching trade." In Broeg's estimation, Brecheen lacked a high, hard fastball, and his curveball did not break at all sharply. Yet for a left-hander he had good control, knew how to vary his delivery from sidearm to three-quarters overhand, and mixed the speed of his pitches from medium fast to slow, slower, and "slowest."

Two extraordinary defensive plays in the first two innings ruined whatever chances the Browns had to stay in the ball game. In the first, after Kreevich singled to left field, Gene Moore walloped a tremendous 365-foot fly into deep right center field. But Hopp came hopping after the ball and, at the last second, managed to snag it on the run with a twisting backhand turn of his glove just inches from the barrier. Kreevich, who had almost reached second by the time the ball was caught, barely got back to first in time to avoid getting doubled up.

When the Cardinals came to bat, Hopp singled, and Musial, the next batter up, smashed Jakucki's fastball, his twelfth pitch, onto the roof of the right field pavilion to put the Redbirds ahead 2 to 0. It was little wonder that announcer Dizzy Dean had begun to call the Cardinals slugger "Musical."

In the second inning, the Browns squandered their best scoring chance in the game. With one down, McQuinn singled for his sixth hit of the series, and then dashed around to third on Christman's single to right. But Hayworth hit a grounder to Kurowski at third for a double play, and the Browns were stopped dead in their tracks. After that, as Drebinger reported in the *New York Times*, "The plucky but outplayed American Leaguers kept pecking away, inning after inning, but making no more headway than a fellow running in a sand pile."

In the third inning, Musial struck again, outrunning the throw to first base after an infield hit. Walker Cooper then whacked a solid single to left for one run; and when Gutteridge allowed Ray Sanders's sharp grounder to shoot right through him for an error, Cooper crossed the base to put the Cardinals ahead by four runs, 4 to 0. Jakucki managed to finish the

Stan Musial crosses the plate after hitting his only career World Series homer. Musial's blast came in game 4 against Sig Jakucki. (Arteaga Photos)

inning, but was replaced by a pinch hitter when the Browns came up to bat. Left hander Al Hollingsworth took over as pitcher, but was the victim in the sixth inning of another Cardinals run after Sanders, on base with a single, was driven home when Marion doubled. Just before he hit his two-bagger, Marion added to the Browns' misery when a foul tip off his bat hit first-string catcher Hayworth in the thigh and put him out of the game.

The Cardinals battered Hollingsworth even more brutally in the seventh, when the National Leaguers came up with two singles, a double, and a pass, all the while failing to score another run. In the eighth, finally, the Browns managed to break through for their lone tally of the afternoon. Moore walked to open the inning. Chet Laabs, who had singled in the fourth and doubled in the sixth, then came up to bat. The man responsible for putting the Browns into the Series hit a sharp grounder to long-armed Marty Marion at shortstop. A lightning-fast double play retired the side, but Moore scored.

Tex Shirley was sent in to replace Hollingsworth, but the Cardinals continued to pound their opponents, with Hopp singling, Musial dropping a double into left field for his third hit of the afternoon, and Walker Cooper getting a walk to fill the bases. After Sanders hit a harmless infield pop-up, Kurowski slammed a tremendous clout to left center, which Kreevich hauled down just in front of the bleacher wall.

In the ninth Cooper unloaded a powerful drive over Kreevich's head in dead center field. The ball, dubbed "the hardest hit ball of the first four games" by the *Sporting News*, struck the fence on the first bounce, 425 feet from the plate. "Perhaps never in Series play has one seen such great effort made for naught," Drebinger in the *Times* drolly reported. "For while the Browns were frantically trying to retrieve the ball to the infield, Cooper kept tearing around the bases, only to overreach himself when he tried to complete the circuit for a homer." The man who had barely managed to complete a 75-yard dash against rookie Ed Bailey years before in Cincinnati "was thrown out by yards at the plate so that all he got was the exercise."

Finally, said Drebinger's colleague Arthur Daley, the World Series at two games apiece had returned to normal, "and the actors in this tense and fantastic drama began to follow the script. The Cardinals looked like the aristocratic champions of old. They hit with their old-time authority, got the pitching they've come to expect, and were completely dominant." Though the Browns acquitted themselves reasonably well for a losing team, the game's result—a 5 to 1 victory for the Cardinals—was just exactly what everyone had expected the Series would produce every day.

The fifth game of the series was a tale of two homers. The fans—many of whom had shown up wearing overcoats on a partly sunny but chilly day—witnessed a masterful pitching duel between Denny Galehouse and Mort Cooper, facing each other for the second time in the Series. Galehouse, Broeg remarked, "threw only two pitches he regretted, a slider and a fastball, both of which cleared the Sportsman's Park right field barrier for home runs."

The Browns had entered the contest confident that the cool-headed Galehouse, who had been the victor over Cooper in the opening game on the previous Wednesday, would repeat his performance over the Redbirds' strapping right-hander. This time Cooper turned the tables, even though Galehouse was to yield only six hits.

The game remained a scoreless deadlock until the sixth inning when Sanders, the Cardinals' rangy first baseman, blasted a prodigious shot that cleared the right field pavilion to put the Cardinals ahead. Litwhiler's even mightier homer came in the eighth, when he sent the ball soaring deep into the pavilion in right center beyond the protective screening, with a carry of more than 400 feet.

In striking out 12 batters, Cooper missed by only one the Series record of 13 set by Howard Ehmke of the Philadelphia Athletics against the Chicago Cubs back in 1929. Galehouse did nearly as well, whiffing 10 and, together with Cooper, setting a new World Series record of 22 strike-outs for a single game. The previous mark of 21 was set by the Cubs and the Chicago White Sox in the first one-city World Series in 1906 and tied by the Athletics and Cubs in 1929. In a final flourish, Cooper struck out the side in the ninth. All three batters—Milt Byrnes, Chet Laabs, and Mike Chartak—were pinch hitters. The occasion also marked the first time in a Series that three pinch hitters struck out in succession. Musial earned the unusual distinction of committing the first Cardinal error of the Series when he fumbled Ray Hayworth's hot single in the fifth.

After the game, as the husky Cooper shuffled off the mound, the crowd gave him an enthusiastic standing ovation. Only later was it revealed that he had hurled the last five innings with a painfully sprained right ankle. He had sustained the injury in the fourth inning while leaping for a bounding ball hit by Al Zarilla, which Cooper had converted into a third out with a quick toss to first base. When he came down on the ground, he badly wrenched his ankle but decided to carry on despite the pain. Catcher Walker Cooper made sure his brother got the last ball pitched, jamming it into his pocket and handing it over to Mort in the clubhouse.

Ziggy Sears, the National League plate umpire for the game, called the pitching of both Galehouse and Cooper the best he had ever seen. "I've been in baseball 35 years," he told the *Sporting News*, "and in the National League since 1935. That was a masterful performance by both men. Cooper had perfect control of his assortment—a forkball, a screwball, and a fastball. Galehouse was brilliant in his effort, too. They did not voice one complaint on my decisions on balls and strikes."

Monday, October 9, was a bleak fall day "more suggestive of football" than baseball, the *St. Louis Star-Times* reported, as the two teams gathered for what was to be the final contest of the Series. The crowd, slow in arriving, was already shivering, and by noon there were still large empty sections in the bleachers and pavilion—owing partly to the fact that this was a workday. Many of the fans had brought blankets. For the first time, there were no long lines at the ticket windows. For the sixth game, the Cardinals and Browns again switched dugouts, with the Redbirds donning their "home" white flannels and assuming the role of host team.

On that same day, British prime minister Winston Churchill was meeting in secret with Soviet premier Josef Stalin in Moscow, following an earlier conference with President Roosevelt at his home in Hyde Park, New York. In every theater of the war, the Allied forces were meeting with success. The U.S. First Army had drawn to within a mile and a half of Aachen, where the German garrison was virtually isolated. In France, Allied forces were also slowly advancing as German forces continued to fall back. In New York, Wendell L. Willkie, who four years earlier had lost the battle for the White House to Franklin Delano Roosevelt and who had been seeking the Republican nomination for president once again, lay in state in the Fifth Avenue Presbyterian Church. Willkie, just fifty-two, had suffered a fatal heart attack on October 6.

Umpiring behind the plate was George Pipgras, who was behind the plate the day when legend says that Babe Ruth pointed to the bleachers and hit a home run off Charlie Root of the Chicago Cubs.

Apparently, the Browns were hot-weather performers, said the *Sporting News*, "but with the mercury dipping to 54, the Browns cooled off." The game matched southpaw Max Lanier for the Cardinals against Nelson Potter, the Browns' top hurler. Neither was in the game when it ended, with Potter the first to go. Incongruous as it seemed, said Broeg in *Leatherneck*, it was a wild pitch by Lanier, the winning pitcher, that gave the victory to the Redbirds.

The Browns got off to a fast start. In the first inning, Lanier fanned three batters in a row, but in the second, Laabs sent a fast ball soaring over Johnny Hopp's head to the 422-foot marker in deepest center field for a triple. Then McQuinn bounced the first pitch over second base for a single, scoring Laabs.

In the third, the Browns threatened again. With two men out, Kreevich dropped a double into center field. Hopp, who had made such a miraculous catch in the fourth game, just missed this time, and then overran the ball. But after Lanier cautiously passed Moore, he held Stephens to a ground ball, which Marion effortlessly scooped up to retire the side.

Finally, in the bottom of the third, the Cardinals launched an attack, with Verban plunking a single into center, then Lanier sending a low drive into the same territory. Kreevich momentarily got his hands on the ball but dropped it, and the Cardinals now had runners on both first

Cardinals' Marty Marion played the entire World Series with a case of the flu.
(National Baseball Hall of Fame Library, Cooperstown NY)

and second. Potter managed to keep the Redbirds in check momentarily, fanning both Litwhiler and Hopp.

In the fourth, the Cardinals resumed the offensive. After Potter retired Musial for the first out, he passed Walker Cooper—and then the Browns' troubles began. Sanders hit a single to center that sent the Cardinals pitcher to third. Kurowski then grounded to shortstop Stephens, and for a fleeting moment it looked as if a double play would get Potter out of his jam. But Stephens's throw pulled Gutteridge off the bag, Cooper scored, two men stood on first and second, and Stephens was charged with an error. Verban then slammed a single into left field for his second hit of the game to drive in Sanders. Lanier followed with another single into center as Kurowski galloped home for the third run of the inning. Bob Muncrief, who had relieved Potter in the second game, then went to the mound for the Browns.

In the sixth inning, with the score standing 3 to 1, the Browns seemed poised for a counterattack. With one down, Laabs drew a pass, and so did McQuinn. With two right-handed batters, Christman and Hayworth, next at bat, Southworth halted the game to talk to Lanier. The pitcher assured his manager that he felt just fine. Allowed to stay in the game, Lanier hitched up his belt, and fired a wild pitch—*the* wild pitch—that sent Laabs to third, Hayworth to second, and Lanier to the dugout. Southworth rushed out to the mound, took the ball from his pitcher, and beckoned for Ted Wilks to come in from the bullpen.

"Lanier, angered, threw his glove into the dugout," Broeg reported, "but that was nothing to what Wilks, batted out in less than three innings in the third game, threw at the Browns. The freshman right-hander stopped the Browns without a run, as Luke Sewell ignored the opportunity to call upon his left-handed pinch-hitters. Christman grounded to Whitey Kurowski, whose accurate throw to the plate caught Laabs coming in standing up, and then Hayworth flied to center field."

After Wilks struck out the last two men to face him in the top of the ninth, the game was over, and the St. Louis Cardinals were the world's champions, winning their fifth title in eight Series and tying the Philadelphia Athletics and Boston Red Sox for second place in winning the most blue ribbons. Only the New York Yankees, with ten championship pennants to their credit, had more.

"The bubble burst today for the Brownies," Daley wrote in the *New York Times*. "Their admirable fight of the past three weeks was at an end, and it was a forlorn, bedraggled-looking ball club which lost out to the

Cardinals in the final game of the World Series. Cinderella was back in shabby garb after a glorious whirl that carried her to her first American League championship."

Yet Sewell deserved "a brisk pat on the back," Daley conceded, "for even getting his odd assortment of talent in the classic. No man ever did so much with so little."

"Fact is," Musial later dryly observed, "the Browns wound up with a .182 team average for the Series. Yet I salute them as an inferior team that just wouldn't quit." Stan the Man was modest about his own achievement during the Series, saying, "I hit .304 in that Series, but, like many a batting champion, including greater ones like Ty Cobb, Rogers Hornsby, and Ted Williams, I never was a World Series standout. I'm just thankful I never was a Series bust, either."

In Musial's analysis, the Cardinals' chief advantage over the Browns was in fielding, and particularly the superiority of Marty Marion at shortstop over his Browns counterpart, Vern Stephens. "There had been some static during the regular season in St. Louis about which was the better," Musial remembered. "Marty didn't have Stephens' power, of course, but his edge afield, as he proved in the Series, was decisive. Marion was brilliant defensively, but Stephens committed three errors."

Fifteen records were set and ten tied in the forty-first World Series in St. Louis. One of the most impressive marks was the forty-nine strikeouts by Cardinals' pitchers, a record for a six-games series. The record stood until Kansas City Royals pitchers tied the mark in 1980. Mike Kreevich of the Browns was the big winner in the record department, setting two new marks and tying two others. Curiously not a single player even attempted to steal a base during the entire Series.

Southworth had to fight his way through a mob of well-wishers, including Ford Frick, president of the National League, and Don Barnes, president of the Browns, who were among those pushing forward to congratulate the team.

With the pressure off, the Cardinals were whooping it up in grand traditional style for the dozens of movie cameramen and newspaper photographers who had waited for the kings of baseball to file into their dressing rooms after clinching the World Series. Hundreds of autograph seekers crowded around the entrance to the clubhouse, whistling, shouting, and milling about as they waited for a glimpse of the world champions. Inside, Verban and Mort Cooper grabbed a grinning Southworth and hoisted him onto their shoulders. In the air, he ruffled the hair of any player who came within reach to the accompaniment of bright flashes and cries from cameramen for those in front to get out of the way.

Through it all, Marty Marion was smiling broadly as people told him he was by far the outstanding player in the Series.

"Aw, shucks, there was nothing to it," was his modest reply. "Everybody did his share."

During the night, a doctor had visited Marion and diagnosed the feverish shortstop with a mild case of flu. But by morning his temperature, which had been as high as 104 during the Series, had finally dropped back to normal.

Later that day a friend phoned Marion and told him, "You won the MVP award." As the Cardinal shortstop later recalled, "I didn't know what the hell it was. I was never too impressed with it at all. That's right. I didn't think about things like that too much. Now, after years have passed that's pretty nice. But back then, it didn't mean a thing to me." More on Marion's mind, perhaps, was his plan to open a clothing store in Reading, Pennsylvania, with Kurowski.

Cardinals president Sam Breadon, a member of the Society for the Preservation of Barbershop Quartets, joined in the victory celebration by singing "I'll Take You Home Again, Kathleen." By the time he finished, quipped Broeg, "everyone wished Kathleen was around to take home."

Reviewing the Series, Sewell told reporters he thought the turning point came in the second game when the Cardinals got two unearned runs and went on to win, 3 to 2, in extra innings.

"Those runs gave them new life," he said. "Without them we would have won the first three games and that would have put us in a swell spot. But we lost and that's all there is to it."

Sewell had been the first outsider to go into the Cardinals' dressing room to congratulate Southworth. The gesture, as Broeg observed, "was symbolic of the clean spirit and good sportsmanship apparent throughout the entire series. There were, with but one exception, no beefs. Neither team engaged in jockeying."

That exception involved Cardinals infielder Emil Verban, who at the start of the Series had gone to see Browns owner Don Barnes to complain that his wife's seat had an obstructed view. "My wife is sitting behind a post," Verban told him, "and I'd like you to do something about it."

But Barnes just laughed and said, "The way you're playing, *you* ought to be sitting behind a post." All of Barnes's friends, who were sitting with him, laughed as well, and Verban was furious. Though the weakest hitter on the Cardinals team, he turned out to be the hitting star of the Series, with a Series average of .412. No doubt his resolve was partly fueled by his anger toward Barnes.

At the end of the final game, Verban walked over to the box seat where Barnes was sitting and said to him, "That'll teach you to put my wife behind a post!"

Barnes himself, when he showed up in the Cardinals' clubhouse to congratulate Southworth, could not help grousing, "You've got one louse on your club. Verban."

Overhearing the exchange, the irrepressible Verban called out to his teammates, "This oughtta cool that Barnes off!"

Largely because of the limited seating capacity at Sportsman's Park, only 206,708 fans saw the 1944 Series. As a result, the winner's share came to only $4,626 per person, the smallest since 1933. Even so, that raised the Cardinals' three-year postseason amount to $15,141, a substantial sum given what most ballplayers earned annually.

On the same day that the Cardinals were celebrating their victory, the War Department, according to the *St. Louis Globe-Democrat*, notified Mrs. Lottie Bumgardner of north St. Louis that her son Arthur Peters had been wounded in action in France. For ten years, Peters had been a clubhouse attendant for both the Cardinals and the Browns, and in 1942 was the Cardinals batboy when they won the World Series.

After the last game, the appreciative Browns management threw a party for the team and their families at the deluxe Chase Hotel. A lavish buffet was spread, and each team member received his World Series share of $2,744. Everyone was there—except for one player. Not surprisingly, the missing athlete was Jakucki. Later in the evening, he finally showed up, drunk and weaving, with dollar bills sticking out of his shirt, sleeves, and ears.

"Now I'm in the money!" he bellowed. Everyone just laughed. Then he disappeared again.

Two days later, Jakucki was found drunk, lying in the street, in a town across the river in Illinois. It was always easier to get alcohol after hours on the east side. He was flat broke and his clothes were filthy. Someone recognized him, got him cleaned up, and brought him back to St. Louis.

The Long Good-bye

After the last game of the Series, the groundskeepers at Sportsman's Park carefully covered the batter's box and the pitcher's mound with canvas. Observers in the stands were heard to ask, "What're they doing that for?" Came the reply: "Why, they're getting ready for the next Streetcar Series, of course." But the Streetcar Series was never again to come to St. Louis, nor would the world of baseball ever see its like again. It was an aberration both of history and of sports, to be celebrated and wondered at, as a marvel of American sportsmanship, patriotism, winning attitude, and maybe just a little boyish innocence and mischief that can be prized and remembered as the best of a long-ago era.

After the 1944 Series ended, Don Barnes sold the Browns to local businessmen Richard Muckerman and his partners, Bill and Charlie DeWitt. Hit by hard financial times, the new ownership was soon forced to sell off the team's best players.

Whether to cut costs, introduce a novelty act, or show their humane side, the new Browns owners put one-armed Pete Gray on the roster as a utility outfielder in 1945, even though by now some of the veteran players were beginning to return from the war. Gray, who had lost his right arm in a truck accident, hit .218 with 13 runs batted in, but he was not popular with his teammates, who thought he hurt their pennant chances. He also took the place of popular Mike Kreevich, whose struggle to overcome alcoholism turned out to be much tougher than winning the pennant. When Gray once asked Sig Jakucki to help him tie his shoes, the irascible pitcher replied, "Tie your own goddamned shoes, you one-armed son of a bitch." In 1945 the Browns finished third, while the Detroit Tigers took the pennant.

Luke Sewell, who had brought respectability to the lovable losers, was fired toward the end of the 1946 season. He went on to manage the

Cincinnati Reds in 1950, 1951, and part of 1952. His Reds teams never managed anything better than a sixth-place finish. He did, however, start a tradition while in Cincinnati that has become commonplace in baseball. It was Sewell who came up with the idea to have the infield dragged in the middle of the game. This interlude not only provided a smoother playing surface, but the longer delay between innings allowed vendors to sell more beer and hot dogs. In 1972 Sewell was persuaded to serve as Ohio chairman for Richard Nixon's reelection campaign. His stay in politics was short-lived after he became disillusioned by the Watergate scandal. Sewell died in 1987 at the age of eighty-six.

For the next three seasons after 1944, Chet Laabs was a part-time player for the Browns and Philadelphia Athletics. He showed that his power spurt at the end of the 1944 season was no fluke by hitting 16 homers and driving in 52 runs in just 80 games for the Browns in 1946. Laabs died in 1983, but to this day his son, Chet, still has the cracked bat that his father used to hit two homers on that memorable October day in 1944 when the Browns won the pennant.

Sig Jakucki was out of baseball by 1945, after finally overstaying his welcome with the Browns. He died in 1979 in Galveston, Texas. His former battery mate, Frank Mancuso, often helped out the troubled Jakucki over the years, occasionally slipping him a $20 bill. After Jakucki died, Mancuso was given a cheap watch by a friend who said he received it from a bartender in Texas. Jakucki had traded the watch at the bar for alcohol.

"Every time I look at it, I think 'I might not have played in the World Series if it wasn't for Jakucki,'" Mancuso told a reporter in 1994.

A month after the 1945 season ended, Cardinals manager Billy Southworth asked team owner Sam Breadon to be released from his contract, which ran for another year, so that he could accept an offer to manage the Boston Braves. He managed the Braves from 1946 to 1951 and took the team to the World Series in 1948. Southworth, who compiled an impressive record of 1,044 wins and 704 losses as a manager, died in 1969. Many baseball fans say he was the greatest manager not yet inducted into the Hall of Fame in Cooperstown, New York.

Marty Marion patrolled shortstop for the Cardinals until 1950, and then managed the team to a third-place finish in 1951. The rival Browns lured Marion back to the playing field part-time as player-manager for the 1952 and 1953 seasons. The eight-time All-Star later moved to Cincinnati and managed the Reds from 1954 through 1956. After leaving the game for a number of years, Marion returned to work for the Cardinals, overseeing operations at the Stadium Club in Busch Stadium for eighteen years.

A month after the 1944 World Series ended, baseball's seventy-eight-year-old commissioner, Kenesaw Mountain Landis, died. During his thirty-five-year tenure, he had strongly opposed gambling-related corruption and shown a remarkable sympathy for the plight of players in many of their disputes with management. But he had sided with the owners in opposing the admittance of black players into the major leagues. No commissioner after Landis was to wield such power and influence. The owners replaced him with Albert "Happy" Chandler, a former Kentucky governor and U.S. senator, and a good ol' boy.

Southworth was replaced by Eddie Dyer, a former Cardinals hurler who had spent twenty years in the Redbirds organization, including directing its AA farm clubs. One of Dyer's first changes as manager was to dispense with Southworth's insistence that the players handle their own luggage and pay for their own transportation to the ballpark. Dyer arranged for the club to take care of such matters and relaxed a few other rules as well, including allowing players to play pinochle—but not poker—in the clubhouse or on the train.

Dyer also had a sudden new wealth of players to work with, now that the war was over. Outfielder Enos Slaughter, infielder Jimmy Brown, and pitchers Murry Dickson and Howie Pollet all returned to the states during the winter of 1945. Some players, though, for a variety of reasons, were unable to return to the squad. Johnny Grodzicki, a hot pitching prospect before the war, had taken two bullets in his thigh during combat and found he could no longer pivot well enough to field a ball.

Dyer and the Cardinals front office wasted little time disposing of the excess manpower they reaped after the war, selling three players to Philadelphia and trading seven to Boston in the first six months of 1946— inspiring some wags to refer to the Braves as the "Cape Cod Cardinals." One of Dyer's most adroit moves was to sell second baseman Jimmy Brown to the Pirates and install versatile utility infielder Albert "Red" Schoendienst at that position. Schoendienst was to become Musial's closest friend on the club and his roommate on the road.

Cardinals outfielder Harry "The Hat" Walker was another player who returned to the team after the war, in 1946, only to have one of his worst seasons ever. After entering the service, he had played ball for the army team in Fort Riley, Kansas, before taking over as manager of the Sixty-fifth Division team in Germany, which captured the European service title after V-E Day. Walker not only saw plenty of baseball, but military action as well, winning the Bronze Star for valor after shooting three German soldiers on a bridge connecting Germany and Austria, and the following day using a .50-caliber machine gun to kill a German patrol. He also received a Purple Heart after being hit with shrapnel.

Walker struggled upon his return to baseball in 1946, hitting just .237, and Breadon quickly traded him to the Phillies. Soon after that, though, Walker found his stride, and in 1947 won the National League batting title with a .363 average. Walker is best known for hitting the ball that scored Enos Slaughter to win the 1946 World Series. After playing for the Phillies, Cubs, and Reds, Walker returned to the Cardinals in 1955, where he finished his career.

Unlike many returning players, Slaughter picked up where he had left off when he joined the Cardinals in 1946, beginning a string of eight consecutive All-Star appearances while hitting .300. Musial, Marion, and other Cardinals remembered him as one of "the greatest hustlers of all times." While he was still in the minors, according to a well-known story, old "Country" was trotting in from right field one day, and by the time he got to the mound he had slowed down to a walk. When he got to the dugout, the manager inquired whether he was too tuckered out to play the rest of the game. Slaughter never walked anywhere after that but always ran—after each grounder, after every fly ball, and even when he drew a base on balls. He was an immensely popular player with the fans and consistently one of the best outfielders in the National League.

That 1946 Series against the Boston Red Sox also gave Slaughter the moment of glory he became best remembered for. After being hit in the elbow during game 5 by Boston's Joe Dobson (an injury that later turned out to be a broken elbow), Slaughter helped win the Series in the seventh and deciding game. With the game tied at 3 in the eighth inning, Slaughter singled. With two men out, Walker then singled on a hit-and-run. Center fielder Leon Culberson threw to the cutoff man, Johnny Pesky, who looked back at Walker. Slaughter, meanwhile, kept hustling and beat the throw home for the winning run.

After his tenth All-Star game in 1953, Slaughter was traded to the Yankees for Bill Virdon and Mel Wright. Demoralized, he then shuttled between New York and Kansas City for the next six seasons, and in 1959 was sold to Milwaukee. He retired after hitting only .171, but in 1985 was elected to the Hall of Fame.

Not long after Musial's return to Donora, following the 1944 World Series, his wife, Lil, gave birth to their second child, Geraldine. Six weeks later, on January 23, 1945, he entered the navy. The Dodgers' Pete Reiser, who was stationed at Fort Riley, Kansas, following his induction into the infantry in 1943, had tried to persuade him to join the army. Harry Walker and Al Brazle were also there, and the base commander's strong interest in developing a competitive squad had resulted in one of the best teams in the service. Other players who had been on the team at one time or another included Murry Dickson, Ken Heintzelman of the Reds, Red Barney of the Dodgers, and Joe Garagiola from the Cardinals farm system. This army team, Reiser told Musial, hardly ever lost.

But Musial's choice of the navy meant that his induction was delayed, allowing him to complete the 1944 season. It also kept him out of combat. Walker, Brazle, and Heintzelman were transferred to the Sixty-fifth Division at Camp Shelby, Mississippi, then shipped overseas, and fought in the Battle of the Bulge—some of the worst fighting of the war—during the winter of 1944–45.

At the naval base in Bainbridge, Maryland, where he was sent for basic training, Musial's head was shaved, like that of all the other inductees, though in his case a photographer was standing by to take Stan the Man's picture.

"Why didn't you tell me who you were?" the barber said apologetically. "I wouldn't have cut it so short."

"Thanks," Musial lamely replied, "but now I know how a guy feels when he's going to the electric chair."

Musial was able to play four or five games at Bainbridge, where two things happened that were to decisively affect his career. By this time, Musial had a reputation as a good defensive outfielder. But the athletic officer at the naval camp, a lieutenant named Jerry O'Brien, put him at first base. Musial was amused, though O'Brien was not.

"Get out of there, Musial!" O'Brien fumed after Musial played first for several games. "You're terrible! You'll never make anybody's team at first base."

The service personnel at Bainbridge also wanted Musial to hit homers as often as possible, so to oblige them Musial slightly altered his batting stance, moving up closer to the plate. "This proved to be an important step in my evolution as a hitter," Musial later agreed.

Eventually he was assigned to Special Services and shipped to Hawaii by way of Treasure Island, the navy's shipping-out point at San Francisco.

In Pearl Harbor, Musial was attached to a ship-repair unit, and also worked on a liberty launch that transferred men and officers from war-damaged aircraft carriers and destroyers to shore. In the afternoons, he was able to maintain his baseball skills by playing ball to entertain soldiers, sailors, marines, and other service-related personnel who crowded into the games.

While Musial was still stationed in Pearl Harbor, his father fell ill with pneumonia a few months after V-J Day. Musial's mother appealed through the Red Cross for an emergency leave for her son, and in January 1946 he finally reached home, after an agonizingly slow journey across the Pacific and then across the continent, to find his father not only still alive but recovering. When his leave was up, Musial was then assigned to the Philadelphia Navy Yard, working as a ship repairman assigned to dismantle a British destroyer. The day before he was to begin working, he walked over to watch some of the men already at work, wearing goggles and heavy gloves and carrying blow torches.

"I realized that a greenpea like me could wind up maiming himself or someone else," he later recalled. "I went to the athletic officer and said: 'Sir, I'm a ship repairman who never has repaired a ship. For my sake and the Navy's, can't you please have my orders changed?' Thanks heavens, he did."

Two months later, Musial was discharged, just in time to play in the 1946 season. Along with a couple of mates from the Pittsburgh area, he decided the fastest way to get home was to hitch a ride along the Pennsylvania Turnpike. While they were standing on the side of the highway in their bellbottoms, a couple of elderly men in a vintage automobile pulled up.

"Gosh, I don't know whether we should get in with these old guys," Musial whispered to one of his fellow swabbies. "It might take us forever to get home."

They climbed in, nevertheless, and soon found themselves speeding down the turnpike at eighty miles per hour. The two men turned out to be members of the Pennsylvania legislature, and when they found out one of their passengers was Musial, they drove up directly to his doorstep in Donora.

By the time he was discharged, Musial had spent most of his fourteen months in the navy playing baseball. "For that he remained grateful and considered himself lucky, a word he often used. Typical of many Americans who confronted the two greatest crises of the 20th century—the

Great Depression and World War II—Musial experienced considerable uncertainty as to what life held for his generation. Seeing the harshness and unfairness of life, he concluded that one had little control over his own fate." Like many men and women of his generation, he believed that God determined a person's talent and fate.

In 1946 Musial acquired his lifelong nickname while on a June road trip to Brooklyn. Whenever he came to the plate against the Dodgers, the fans started chanting, but sportswriter Bob Broeg, who was covering the contest, could not make out the words. After the game, he asked the Cardinals' traveling secretary, Leo Ward, if he could decipher the Brooklyn accent.

"Every time Stan came up," Ward told him, "they chanted, 'Here come the man!' "

" 'That man,' you mean," Broeg replied.

"No, '*the* man,' " Ward explained.

Broeg, now a sportswriter for the *Post-Dispatch*, alluded to the anecdote in his column, and Musial found himself known henceforward as Stan the Man—ironically, a nickname bestowed on him by the Cardinals' fiercest rivals.

That same year, Musial was again voted Most Valuable Player, as he was in 1943. He went on to win the award for a third time in 1948, and to play in more All-Star games than any other player. In 1957 he became the first player in the National League to earn an annual salary of $100,000.

During the 1960 season, Musial was being used primarily as a pinch hitter. During the All-Star game at Yankee Stadium—his first visit to the House That Ruth Built since the 1943 World Series—Stan the Man pinch-hit a Gerry Staley sinker deep into the right field upper deck for a record-breaking sixth All-Star home run. The National League won that game, 6 to 0.

Later that season the Cardinals were locked in a pennant race with the Pittsburgh Pirates, a team Musial had never hit well against. This time he hit a two-run homer in the twelfth inning that ended a Pirates' seven-game winning streak. By now, at Pittsburgh stadium ovations for local hero Musial "had ended as he threatened to short-circuit the Pirates' pennant hopes. He even noted a coolness among his old friends around Donora for his Pirate-bashing." But the Cardinals faded and Musial went into a batting slump, though he still finished the season with a respectable .275 average, 17 home runs, and 63 RBIs. The team finished in third place with an 86-68 record, nine games out of first, as the Pirates clinched the pennant and went on to win the World Series.

Many of Musial's fans now both expected and hoped that he would call it quits. In October, Bob Broeg, Musial's future collaborator on an autobiography, even wrote a piece in *Sport* magazine titled "Goodbye, Stan."

Musial, though, had other thoughts. He wanted to play one more season, and on September 15 announced that he would return to play the following year. He gave five reasons for his decision: he still enjoyed the game, he thought he could help the Cardinals win a pennant in 1961, Cardinals president Bing Devine wanted him back, and he had his eye on certain records. In particular, he wanted to reach two milestones—the number of career hits in the National League, and the total-base record in the major leagues. In just one more season, Musial believed, he could break those records. He accomplished both feats. In the four decades since his retirement, only two men—Hank Aaron and Pete Rose—have surpassed his career hits mark. Only Aaron has more total bases in major-league history. When he retired following the 1963 season, Musial held thirty-three National League records.

New Cardinals owner August Busch III strongly concurred with Musial's and Devine's decision, saying, "After all, Stan is still the greatest Cardinal of them all, and we hope he'll play as long as he's able." Later Musial signed a contract for $75,000, a salary cut of $5,000 from the previous year.

That fall, for the first time, he also got involved in a national political campaign as a high-profile supporter of Democratic candidate John F. Kennedy in the 1960 presidential race. Back in September 1959, Musial had met the handsome, charismatic senator from Massachusetts in front of Milwaukee's Shroeder Hotel, where Kennedy was stumping at the time. Kennedy recognized Musial as one of the men waiting to board a team bus, stuck out his hand, and said, "You're Stan Musial, aren't you? My name is Jack Kennedy. I'm glad to meet you." Then, with a smile, Kennedy added, "They tell me you're too old to play ball and I'm too young to be president, but maybe we'll fool them." A captivated Musial, inspired by Kennedy's vision of a New Frontier for America, especially his call for an end to racial discrimination, became an ardent supporter of the Massachusetts senator.

After his career as a player ended in 1963, Musial served as a senior vice president of the Cardinals organization until 1991. Sportscaster and fellow

St. Louisan Bob Costas once described Musial as more of a consistent player than a flamboyant one like DiMaggio: "He didn't hit a homer in his last at-bat; he hit a single. He didn't hit in 56 straight games. He married his high school sweetheart and stayed married to her, never married a Marilyn Monroe. He didn't play with the sheer joy and style that goes alongside Willie Mays' name. None of those easy things are there to associate with Stan Musial. All Musial represents is more than two decades of sustained excellence and complete decency as a human being."

The Browns played their last game in Sportsman's Park on September 27, 1953, losing 2 to 1 in an eleven-inning game to the Chicago White Sox before a sparse crowd of only 3,174 unusually quiet fans. Former Cardinals shortstop Marty Marion was the Browns manager that season and had even played in three games. Few were surprised when the Browns lost their hundredth game of the season to finish in last place. Nor was there much surprise when owner Bill Veeck announced a few days later that the team had been sold to a group of Baltimore investors. In 1954 the Browns became the Baltimore Orioles.

It was the end of a fifty-two-year relationship between the team and the city. A few disgruntled fans had hung an effigy of Veeck in Sportsman's Park as early as the spring, when word began to leak out that he might be selling the team at the end of the season. But leaving St. Louis was not an overnight decision.

The colorful Veeck had purchased the financially troubled team in 1951, with the goal of running the mighty Cardinals out of town. The current Redbirds owner, Fred Saigh, had been jailed for income-tax evasion, and the timing seemed right to take control of baseball in the city. But Veeck's master plan failed. When it appeared that the franchise might be sold to another city, Augustus Busch III of the Anheuser-Busch family came to the Cardinals' rescue and bought the team for $3,750,000, bringing them back to respectability.

Things continued to spiral downward for Veeck and the Browns, who tried dozens of stunts to raise attendance including "Manage from the Stands" day and the infamous sight of three-foot-seven Eddie Gaedel standing at the plate to lead off a game (he walked). The other owners were less than amused by Veeck's antics and forced him to sell the team to a group from Baltimore.

After the war, Bob Broeg went on to cover the Cardinals for the *St. Louis Post-Dispatch* and eventually became the sports editor of the paper. In 1979 he was inducted into baseball's Hall of Fame. Of all the participants in the 1944 World Series, only he and Musial were to be so honored.

Sportsman's Park survived the Browns' departure, with the Cardinals continuing to play in the stadium until 1966, though it was renamed Busch Stadium in 1953. In 1966 the park was finally abandoned when the Cardinals moved into their new, modern Busch Stadium in downtown St. Louis. Sportsman's Park was later demolished. Today the Herbert Hoover Boys' Club, with a baseball diamond where the major league one used to be, stands on the site.

In October of 1966, when the Baltimore Orioles swept past the Los Angeles Dodgers for the franchise's first World Series title, there was nobody dancing in the streets of St. Louis. Even though the Orioles shut out the National League champions in the final three games, there was no partying upstairs in St. Louis's storied Chase Hotel, the way there had been in 1944. By 1966 the St. Louis Browns were just a ghost story, pushed to the pages of baseball encyclopedias. They lived on now only as tales told by grandparents to grandchildren on hot summer days while watching the Cardinals play.

ACKNOWLEDGMENTS

No book that explores in-depth a historical event that took place sixty-plus years ago gets written without the help of many people. This book is no exception. Our agent, Andrew Blauner, believed in this project from the very beginning, and we cannot thank him enough. Rob Taylor, our editor at the University of Nebraska Press, has been a constant support whose vision has made this book possible. We would also like to thank the entire staff at UNP for all their hard work. And a special thank-you to Ruth Melville, for her diligent copyediting.

Thanks also to John McGuire of the *St. Louis Post-Dispatch*, who has become a good friend and editorial ally in our long quest during the interview and writing process. Bob Broeg proved that he is as generous with his time as he is exemplary as a writer about sports, and we have done our best to follow his example.

Matt Heidenry, Donna Karondo, and the Honerable Thomas C. Grady helped point us in the right direction during our research in various archives in St. Louis. We are also thankful to the staff of the St. Louis Historical Society and of the main branch of the St. Louis Public Library. A particular thank-you to Steve Toman, who provided us with a rare copy of the November 1944 issue of *Leatherneck Magazine Pacific Edition*.

Most of all, we are grateful to those players who shared their memories of the 1944 World Series with us: Marty Marion, the 1944 MVP; Frank Mancuso, Red Hayworth, and Don Gutteridge. Chet Laabs, son of former St. Louis Brown Chet Laabs, was kind enough to relate some stories about his late father, as well as his own childhood memories from 1944.

Bill Francis and Bill Burdick in the research and photo departments of the National Baseball Hall of Fame in Cooperstown, New York, were extremely helpful from the beginning of this project to the end. A special thanks to Brad Arteaga of Arteaga Photos in St. Louis, and to Bob Posen and Leonard Adreon, who also shared their personal memories of the 1944 season with us.

JH & BT

My parents have always been an incredible source of support for me, both personally and professionally, and this project was no exception. I treasure my relationship with them. Special thanks to the following people: Melissa, Jason, and Derek for all of their love and support; my grandparents, Milton and Edna, who are always first in line to read anything I write; Ellen and Steve for their loving support and encouragement throughout this project and always; and Grandma Ruth, who never let a visit go by without asking me how the book was coming; Abigale and David, Glen, Alexis, and Eric (Cuz) for all of their encouragement; Shvinky, for a lifetime's worth of support; Annie and Elizabeth for their unconditional love; finally, to my wife, Emily, and son, Oliver, the two most important people in my life. They are *my* heroes, and my love for them cannot be measured in words.

BT

NOTES

Full publication information for book citations can be found in the sources section.

1. Win One for the Georgia Peach

8   *I wouldn't say*: Heller, *As Good as It Got*, 101.

8   *He was a mean*: Heller, *As Good as It Got*, 101–2.

13   *Sensing the dramatics*: Heller, *As Good as It Got*, 107.

2. Who Are Those Guys?

20   *finally closed down*: In 1985 Union Station reopened as an entertainment/convention complex and hotel.

20   *The Browns came to St Louis*: The Milwaukee Brewers were charter members of the American League in 1901 and finished in last place. The team moved to St. Louis the following season and became the Browns, named after a St. Louis team from the late 1800s named the Brown Stockings. The Browns fared relatively well in some years and badly in others, but were popular with fans. In 1916 the team was sold to Philip Ball, who had owned the old St. Louis Terriers of the defunct Federal League. From the beginning, the Browns struggled under Ball. The one bright spot during Ball's regime came in 1920. In that year, his sixth season in the big leagues, George Sisler batted .407 with record 257 hits. In 1922, under Sisler's leadership, St. Louis almost won the American League pennant. Sisler did his part by batting .420. But the New York Yankees, led by Babe Ruth, edged St. Louis by a single game. Unfortunately for the Browns, Sisler suffered from chronic sinusitis in 1923 and missed the entire season. Though he returned in 1924 and played until 1928, he never again compiled numbers he once had. The Browns floundered over the next decade and hit their low point in the late 1930s. New owner Donald Barnes saw his team draw just 80,922 fans for the entire season in 1936 (compared to the 533,349 fans that turned out in 1924 when Sisler returned to the lineup). Things did not improve: the Browns lost a total of

316 games over the next three years. In fact, during the 1930s St. Louis averaged 95 losses per season. In 1939 the Browns ended the decade by losing 111 games and finishing a staggering 64 ½ games out of first place. That season, Browns pitchers had an earned run average of 6.01 and walked 739 batters, 100 more than the next worst team in all of baseball.

24   *Why don't you get Sewell?*: Luke Sewell, "They Made Me a Cinderella," *Esquire*, July 1945, 86ff.

24   *Even more unusual*: Sewell refers to this novel in his July 1945 article for *Esquire*, but it was apparently never published.

31   *For the 1942 season*: *Look*, May 4, 1943, 70.

31   *Stephens was a more*: Mead, *Baseball Goes to War*, 129.

33   *one of the originators*: Mead, *Baseball Goes to War*, 111–12.

34   *Clary was real good*: Mead, *Baseball Goes to War*, 114.

36   *When he was forced*: Mead, *Baseball Goes to War*, 132.

36   *Sent to Honolulu*: Heller, *As Good As It Got*, 101ff.

38   *Browns vice president*: *Sporting News*, July 7, 1944.

39   *We found it*: Mead, *Baseball Goes to War*, 112.

42   *A Wisconsin board*: Mead, *Baseball Goes to War*, 124.

43   *St. Louis can no more*: Kansas City did get its own franchise in 1969. The Royals won their first American League pennant in 1980 and their first world championship in 1985 when they defeated the St. Louis Cardinals.

43   *Baseball must take heed*: Mead, *Baseball Goes to War*, 125–26.

44   *As one sportswriter*: Kyle Crichton, "The Unbelievable Browns," *Colliers*, September 1944.

44   *Another writer opined*: Crichton, "The Unbelievable Browns."

44   *The Browns' strength*: Mead, *Baseball Goes to War*, 141.

47   *He had plenty*: Mead, *Baseball Goes to War*, 137.

49   *had guts*: Crichton, "The Unbelievable Browns."

51   *That's why damn near*: Golenbock, *The Spirit of St. Louis*, 296.

51   *the most underrated player*: Golenbock, *The Spirit of St. Louis*, 296.

51   *But something like*: Golenbock, *The Spirit of St. Louis*, 296.

52   *As the Browns struggled*: Mark Neilsen, "The Streetcar Series," *St. Louis Magazine*, April 1978, 96–97.

3. The Half-Apple Curve

56   *He quickly noticed*: Broeg, *Bob Broeg*, 139.

57   *We were always kidding*: Golenbock, *The Spirit of St. Louis*, 251.

61   *Back in our day*: Heller, *As Good As It Got*, 110.

61   *Goddamn*: Heller, *As Good As It Got*, 110.

63   *But Galehouse*: Heller, *As Good As It Got*, 112.

72   *He found the ballpark*: Berkow, *Red: A Biography of Red Smith*, 48.

4. The Empire Strikes Back

79   *Marty, you're my best friend*: Golenbock, *The Spirit of St. Louis*, 252.

80   *they bested them in quality*: Mead, *Baseball Goes to War*, 142.

81   *Do you know why*: Golenbock, *The Spirit of St. Louis*, 254.

83   *Particularly after a night game*: Golenbock, *The Spirit of St. Louis*, 256.

85   *Common sense had to tell*: Golenbock, *The Spirit of St. Louis*, 260.

85   *he was sneaky fast*: Golenbock, *The Spirit of St. Louis*, 252.

85   *One player that Southworth*: Golenbock, *The Spirit of St. Louis*, 261.

86   *In doing so*: Ironically, the St. Louis Cardinals actually started out as the St. Louis Browns. In 1892, one year after the American Association folded, the St. Louis Browns joined the National League as one of the twelve original teams. In 1899 the Browns were purchased by Frank and Stanley Robison, renamed the St. Louis Perfectos, and given new white uniforms with red trim and socks. After fans began remarking about the "lovely shade of cardinal" of the uniforms, a nickname was unofficially born. One year later, in 1900, the name was officially changed and the team became the St. Louis Cardinals. After fifteen years of little success, the team was sold to lawyer James C. Jones and a group of stockholders, including a St. Louis automobile dealer named Sam Breadon. One major problem was that the team lacked leadership. That leadership arrived in the person of young Branch Rickey, who was appointed president of the Cardinals in 1917. He held that position until 1920, when he was named vice president, general manager, and manager. At the same time, Breadon became majority stockholder and president. St. Louis's star player at the time was Rogers Hornsby, who dominated the National League, including winning the triple crown in 1922. That year he batted .401. Two seasons later, in 1924, he batted .424. In 1925 he again won the triple crown. The following season, he performed as a player/manager when Rickey moved exclusively to the front office. The move paid off for St. Louis, which defeated the New York Yankees to win its first World Series title. Six years later, in 1932, rookie pitcher Dizzy Dean won eighteen games, leading the league in strikeouts, shutouts, and innings pitched. In 1934 Dean won thirty games and led the Cardinals, known as the "Gashouse Gang," to the pennant on the final day of the season. The team then went on to win the World Series over the Detroit Tigers. In 1942, the first war season, the Cardinals stormed from behind in the final third of the season, erasing a 10 ½ game deficit over the final 51 games. Led by Enos Slaughter and rookie Stan Musial, they then defeated the Yankees for the world championship. The following season, Musial won the MVP award, leading the National League in seven offensive categories, but the Cardinals lost in the World Series to their now familiar rivals, the Yankees.

87   *I guarantee ya*: Golenbock, *The Spirit of St. Louis*, 262.

89   *Don't laugh at me*: Musial, *Stan Musial*, 22.

90   *Martin then dropped*: Musial, *Stan Musial*, 60.

93   *You can see why*: Bob Broeg, *Leatherneck*, Pacific ed., November 1944.

95   *I realize it's asking*: *Sporting News*, October 12, 1944.

5. Young Man Musial

100   *stained by perennial smog*: Musial, *Stan Musial*, 9.

101   *As a teenager*: Musial, *Stan Musial*, 5.

101   *a job so brutal*: Musial, *Stan Musial*, 6.

102   *My brother Ed*: Musial, *Stan Musial*, 7.

104   *A few days later*: Musial, *Stan Musial*, 10.

104   *Red-faced and embarrassed*: Musial, *Stan Musial*, 25.

105   *a good ol' country boy*: Golenbock, *The Spirit of St. Louis*, 253

105   *nobody could throw*: Golenbock, *The Spirit of St. Louis*, 253.

106   *didn't have a good arm*: Golenbock, *The Spirit of St. Louis*, 253.

106   *Tell you the kind of kid*: Golenbock, *The Spirit of St. Louis*, 253.

107   *during the war years*: Giglio, *Musial*, 83.

6. War Games

110   *But baseball had a special*: Mead, *Baseball Goes to War*, 82.

111   *and accused President Roosevelt*: Mead, *Baseball Goes to War*, 88.

112   *In boxing*: Mead, *Baseball Goes to War*, 90.

113   *Four aged players hobbled*: Mead, *Baseball Goes to War*, 92.

113   *Perhaps the baseball man*: Mead, *Baseball Goes to War*, 95.

114   *an honor that*: Mead, *Baseball Goes to War*, 86.

115   *so loaded with past*: Scheller, "The National Pastime Enlists," 7.

115   *The greatest baseball season*: Creamer, *Baseball in '41*, 9.

115   *Early in 1941*: Scheller, "The National Pastime Enlists," 12.

115   *Two months later*: Scheller, "The National Pastime Enlists," 14.

116   *Golfer Porky Oliver*: Scheller, "The National Pastime Enlists," 20.

117   *endured constant criticism*: Scheller, "The National Pastime Enlists," 26.

119   *The major leagues grandly*: Mead, *Baseball Goes to War*, 74.

120   *Cracker Jacks*: Mead, *Baseball Goes to War*, 76.

121   *But alarms went off*: Mead, *Baseball Goes to War*, 78.

121   *the fans were thought to prefer*: Mead, *Baseball Goes to War*, 78.

121   *the plight of old-time players*: Mead, *Baseball Goes to War*, 78.

123   *problems for minor-league baseball*: Finoli, *Good of the Country*, 142.

123   *The majors would then*: Finoli, *Good of the Country*, 142.

124   *A minor-league teenage sensation*: Finoli, *Good of the Country*, 144.

125   *The beach was plenty hot*: Finoli, *Good of the Country*, 150.

125   *The first time he went in*: Richard Goldstein, "When the Boys of Summer Were the Boys of Winter," *New York Times*, March 16, 2004.

8. Midnight Strikes

140 *There had been some static*: Musial, *Stan Musial*, 82.

142 *Two days later*: Golenbock, *The Spirit of St. Louis*, 308.

9. The Long Good-bye

147 *But Musial's choice*: Musial, *Stan Musial*, 96.

148 *I realized that a greenpea*: Musial, *Stan Musial*, 83.

148 *For that he remained grateful*: Musial, *Stan Musial*, 95.

149 *had ended as he threatened*: Musial, *Stan Musial*, 248.

SOURCES

Books

Berkow, Ira. *Red: A Biography of Red Smith.* New York: Times Books, 1986.

Borst, Bill. *The Best of Seasons: The 1944 St. Louis Cardinals and St. Louis Browns.* Jefferson NC: McFarland, 1995.

Broeg, Bob. *Bob Broeg: Memories of a Hall of Fame Sportswriter.* Champaign IL: Sagamore, 1995.

Creamer, Robert W. *Baseball in '41: A Celebration of the Best Baseball Season Ever—in the Year America Went to War.* New York: Viking, 1991.

Finoli, David. *For the Good of the Country: World War II Baseball in the Major and Minor Leagues.* Jefferson NC: McFarland, 2002.

Giglio, James N. *Musial: From Stash to Stan the Man.* Columbia: University of Missouri Press, 2001.

Gilbert, Thomas. *Baseball at War: World War II and the Fall of the Color Line.* New York: Franklin Watts, 1997.

Goldstein, Richard. *Spartan Seasons: How Baseball Survived the Second World War.* New York: Macmillan, 1980.

Golenbock, Peter. *The Spirit of St. Louis: A History of the St. Louis Cardinals and Browns.* New York: HarperCollins, 2000.

Heller, David Alan. *As Good As It Got: The 1944 St. Louis Browns.* Charleston SC: Arcadia, 2003.

Lansche, Jerry. *Stan the Man Musial: Born to Be a Ballplayer.* Dallas: Taylor, 1994.

Mead, William B. *Baseball Goes to War: Stars Don Khaki, 4-Fs Vie for Pennant.* New York: Farragut, 1985.

Musial, Stan, as told to Bob Broeg. *Stan Musial: The Man's Own Story.* New York: Doubleday, 1964.

Scheller, Jason. "The National Pastime Enlists: How Baseball Fought the Second World War." M.A. thesis, Texas Tech University, 2002.

Publications

The 1944 coverage of spring training, the regular season, and the World Series in the following newspapers have been used throughout: *Cape Girardeau Southeast Missourian, Donora (PA) Herald-American, New York Times, New York Daily News, New York Post, St. Louis Globe-Democrat, St. Louis Post-Dispatch, St. Louis Star-Times, Sporting News.*

Specific articles in *Collier's, Esquire, Leatherneck, Life, Look,* and *St. Louis Magazine* are cited in the footnotes.

INDEX

Breadon, Sam (*cont.*)
clubs in St. Louis, 42–43; and Stan
Musial, 98–100, 106–7
Brecheen, Harry: in the first game of
the 1944 World Series, 58, 61; in the
fourth game of the 1944 World Series,
133; in the second game of the 1944
World Series, 79, 80, 83; talent of, 85
Bricker, John W., 73
Broeg, Bob: honors awarded to, 151–52;
on Stan Musial, 149, 150; on the 1944
World Series, 56–58, 64–65, 69, 93,
96, 129, 131, 133, 135, 137, 139, 141
Broeg, Dorth, 56–57
Brooklyn Dodgers, the, 5, 18, 80, 105,
106, 129; Branch Rickey of, 20, 43;
failures during the 1944 season, 90;
and Larry MacPhail, 113–14; Leo
Durocher of, 68, 115, 126; loss of
players to the military, 85, 147; loss
to the St. Louis Cardinals, 57, 108;
spring training location, 119, 120;
Tommy Brown of, 124
Brown, Jimmy, 145
Brown, Tommy, 124
Brown, Virgil, 39
Brown Shoes, 19
Bumgardner, Lottie, 142
Bunardzya, Johnny, 103
Busch, August, III, 150, 151
Busch, Gussie, 87
Busch Stadium, 152
Byerly, George, 93
Bynes, Milt, 10
Byrnes, Milt, 39, 41, 44, 46, 136; in the
first game of the 1944 World Series,
77

Cairo IL, 78, 119
Camilli, Dolph, 85
Campbell, Raymond, 39
Cape Girardeau MO, 32, 58–59, 119
Cape Girardeau Southeast Missourian, 59,
78
Caretti, M. M., 118
Carlson, H. C., 103

Carson, Ed, 107–8
Carson, Sue, 107–8
Case, George, 11
Casey, Hugh, 129
Caster, George, 44, 46
Chandler, Albert, 145
Chandler, Spud, 45, 47
Chartak, Mike, 46, 136
Chicago Bears, the, 9
Chicago Black Sox, the, 66
Chicago Cubs, the, 18, 58, 65, 119, 136,
146
Chicago White Sox, the, 3, 5, 18, 32, 56,
71, 136, 151; media coverage of, 46;
spring training location, 119, 120
Christman, Mark, 5, 10, 11–12, 33, 34; as
an older player, 44; in the first game
of the 1944 World Series, 74–76; in
the fourth game of the 1944 World
Series, 139; in the second game of the
1944 World Series, 91–96; talent of,
46, 60; in the third game of the 1944
World Series, 130; on Vern Stephens,
52; war-plant job of, 36
Christman, Virginia, 33
Christopher, Russ, 51
Churchill, Winston, 7, 137
Cincinnati Reds, the, 114, 119, 122, 124,
144, 146, 147
Clary, Ellis, 8, 9–10, 34, 36, 44, 50; on
Jack Kramer, 52; and Mike Kreevich,
51; on the St. Louis Cardinals, 61
Cleveland Indians, the, 4, 25, 125; Bob
Feller of, 117; spring training location,
119, 120; Stan Musial and, 104
Clift, Harlond, 34, 49
Cobb, Ty, 3, 53, 54, 140
Cochrane, Mickey, 37
Cogan, W. J., 47–48
Considine, Bob, 67
Coombs, Cecil, 95
Cooper, Mort, 36; after winning the 1944
World Series, 140–41; and Danny
Litwhiler, 81; in the first game of the
1944 World Series, 58, 61, 70, 74, 76;

in the fourth game of the 1944 World Series, 135–36; media coverage of, 62; pitching talent of, 73; playing style of, 89–90; salary of, 83; talent of, 78–79, 86

Cooper, Walker, 80; in the first game of the 1944 World Series, 58, 60–61, 61, 74–75; in the fourth game of the 1944 World Series, 133–36, 139; playing style of, 89–90; in the second game of the 1944 World Series, 91; talent of, 96, 108; in the third game of the 1944 World Series, 128–30

Cooper Union Institute of Technology, 121–22

Costas, Bob, 151

Courtney, Del, 52

Cracker Jacks, 120

Creamer, Robert, 115; *Baseball in '41*, 115

Crosby, Bing, 44

Crosetti, Frank, 10, 13, 45, 124

Culberson, Leon, 146

Daley, Arthur, 37, 91–92, 96, 97, 131, 135, 139–40

Daniel, Dan, 14, 49, 62, 80

David, Bummy, 116

D-day, 6–7, 125

Dean, Dizzy, 66, 73, 133, 157

Detroit Tigers, the, 2, 4, 5, 11, 13, 51, 53, 54, 57, 59, 131, 143; Hank Greenberg of, 2, 115, 117, 118; spring training location, 119

Devine, Bing, 150

DeWitt, Bill, 5, 36, 41, 47, 57; on having two major league clubs in St. Louis, 42–43; ownership of the St. Louis Browns by, 143; recruitment of Luke Sewell by, 24, 25, 33, 55; recruitment of players by, 34; recruitment of Sigmund Jakucki by, 38; and Vern Stephens, 52

DeWitt, Charlie, 143

Dickey, Bill, 2, 45

Dickson, Murry, 79, 80, 145, 147

DiMaggio, Joe, 2, 18, 23, 37, 45, 48, 105,

151; military service of, 110, 116, 118; and popularity of baseball, 115

Dobson, Joe, 146

Doerr, Bobby, 2

Donnelly, Blix, 61, 70, 93–95, 127

Donora Herald-American, 103, 107

Dotson, Dotty, 52

draft, the, 42, 45, 47, 107; age of men eligible for, 111–12; Selective Service System (sss) code, 110–11, 123. *See also* military, the

Drebinger, John, 14, 59, 73, 77, 96, 127, 129, 133, 135

Dunkley, Charles, 67

Dunn, Tom, 127–28

Durocher, Leo, 68, 115, 126, 129

Dyer, Eddie, 99, 145

Earnshaw, George, 65

Eastman, Joseph B., 118–19

Echo, 46

Ehmke, Howard, 65, 136

Erskine, Carl, 106

Etten, Nick, 1, 10, 13, 126

Europe during World War II, 6–7

Falls, Joe, 4

fans: fights between, 69; St. Louis Browns, 5–6, 13–14, 15, 23–24, 48–49, 59, 65–66, 68, 87, 108–9, 130–31, 151, 155–56; St. Louis Cardinals, 23, 65–66, 68; torn between both teams, 70; at the 1944 World Series, 65–66, 69–71, 70, 130–31, 132, 136–37, 142

Feller, Bob, 4, 117

Felsh, Arthur, 68

Ferrell, Rick, 46, 49

first game of the 1944 World Series, 74–77

football, 43

Fort Worth Cats, 95

fourth game of the 1944 World Series, 132–40

French, Andrew J., 102

French, Larry, 125

Frick, Ford, 17, 140

57; career after the 1944 World Series, 144; fighting by, 8, 36, 37–38, 143; in the fourth game of the 1944 World Series, 133–34; pitching talent of, 46, 50; playing for the Honolulu Braves, 36–37; recruited by Bill DeWitt, 38; various teams of, 36–37

Johnson, Billy, 45
Jones, Earl, 36
Jones, James C., 157
Jurisch, Al, 61, 130

Kansas City Royals, the, 140
Kaufmann, Aloys P., 47
Kaufmann, Tony, 95
Keller, Charlie, 2, 45
Kennedy, John F., 150
Kiles, Charles, 67
Klein, Lou, 59
Kloz, Helen, 103
Kramer, Jack, 7, 41, 44, 46, 87; family relationships of, 52; media coverage of, 62; in the 1944 season opener, 47; talent of, 47; in the third game of the 1944 World Series, 128–31
Kreevich, Mike, 5, 10, 13, 14, 29, 46, 54, 65; alcohol use by, 32–33, 41, 51, 143; as an older player, 44; in the first game of the 1944 World Series, 74, 76; in the fourth game of the 1944 World Series, 133, 137; records set by, 140; in the 1944 season opener, 47; in the second game of the 1944 World Series, 91–96, 93; in the third game of the 1944 World Series, 130
Krist, Howie, 80
Kurowski, Whitey, 60–61, 76, 80, 84, 141; in the fourth game of the 1944 World Series, 135, 139; in the second game of the 1944 World Series, 96; talent of, 85; in the third game of the 1944 World Series, 129–30

Laabs, Chester, 3–4, 5, 144
Laabs, Chet, 1, 2, 3–5, 10, 18, 34, 46, 65; as an older player, 44; career after the

1944 World Series, 144; in the first game of the 1944 World Series, 74–76; in the fourth game of the 1944 World Series, 134, 136, 139; homeruns hit by, 12–13, 54; media coverage of, 17, 95; in the second game of the 1944 World Series, 91; in the third game of the 1944 World Series, 128; war-plant job of, 36, 124

Labash, Lillian. See Musial, Lillian
La Guardia, Fiorello, 73
Lancos, Mary, 100–101
Landis, Kenesaw Mountain: and black players, 43; death of, 145; and Eddie Grant, 114; order regarding baseball manufacturing, 121; order regarding part-time players, 124; order regarding spring training, 118–19; order regarding the St. Louis Cardinals and minor league clubs, 103; and possible closure of baseball during World War II, 116; scandals surrounding, 66
Lanier, Hubert Max, 61, 78–79, 80, 85; in the fourth game of the 1944 World Series, 137; in the second game of the 1944 World Series, 91–93
Leatherneck, 57, 93, 129, 133, 137
Lee, Josh, 112
Leonard, Dutch, 11, 126
Life, 66
Lindell, Johnny, 1, 10, 11, 13, 54, 96; and U. S. O. shows, 126
Litwhiler, Danny, 17, 61, 107; army tours of, 106; in the fourth game of the 1944 World Series, 135–36, 139; recruitment by the St. Louis Cardinals, 80–83; talent of, 85; in the third game of the 1944 World Series, 128
Look, 66
Los Angeles Angels, the, 123
Los Angeles Dodgers, the, 152

MacArthur, Douglas, 41, 47
Mack, Connie, 60, 64–65
MacPhail, Larry, 113–14

Majeski, Hank, 45

Mancuso, Frank, 10, 44, 46; health problems of, 39, *40*; help given to Sigmund Jakucki by, 144; in the second game of the 1944 World Series, 93

Mancuso, Gus, 46

Marion, Marty, 146; assessment of the St. Louis Browns, 86–87; background of, 87–89; career after the 1944 World Series, 144–45, 151; in the first game of the 1944 World Series, 57–61, 72–73, 76; in the fourth game of the 1944 World Series, 134, 137; 4-F status of, 80; illness during the World Series, 87, *138*, 141; modesty of, 141; and Mort Cooper, 79; salary of, 83; in the second game of the 1944 World Series, 91–96, 93; and Stan Musial, 105, 106, 107; talent of, 140; in the third game of the 1944 World Series, 130

Martin, Herschel, 2, 10, 11

Martin, Johnny L., 78

Martin, Pepper, 74, 90

Mays, Willie, 151

McCarthy, Joe, 1, 15, 120

McGinty, Jack, 102

McNutt, Paul V., 112–13

McQuinn, George, 5, 10, 11, 13, 17, 31, 33; as an older player, 44; in the first game of the 1944 World Series, 74–76; in the fourth game of the 1944 World Series, 133, 137; military physicals of, 42; in the second game of the 1944 World Series, 95–96; and Sigmund Jakucki, 50–51; splits the winning ball with Sigmund Jakucki, 14–15; talent of, 46, 60; in the third game of the 1944 World Series, 129–31; wins against Cleveland, 50

McQuinn, Kathleen Baker, 33

Mead, William B., 110, 121; *Baseball Goes to War*, 110, 121

media coverage: of athletes in the mil-

itary, 114, 117–18; of Chet Laabs, 17, 95; of the New York Yankees, 46; of Sportsman's Park, 72; of the St. Louis Browns, 14, 15, 17, 18, 38, 44, 46–47, 47–48, 52, 58, 62, 64; of the St. Louis Cardinals, 46, 59, 93, 151–52; of the 1944 World Series, 66–67, 69–70, 91–92, 95, 96–97, 127, 129, 131

Merullo, Lennie, 49

Metheny, Bud, 10, 49

Methodist Board of Temperance, 112

Milan, Clyde, 11

military, the: alcohol sales and, 112; baseball games between army and navy, 125; baseball writers in, 57–58, 67; black soldiers in, 43–44; boxers in, 113, 117; draft, 42, 45, 47, 107; and 4-F status men, 44–45, 80, 114; leaves given to athletes, 116; players returning to baseball from, 124, 145–46; Selective Service System (SSS), 110–11, 123; St. Louis Browns players and, 33, 38, 44, 68–69, 147–49; and U. S. O. shows, 125–26. *See also* World War II

Milnar, Al, 46

Milosevich, Mike, 49

Milwaukee WI, 20

Milwaukee Brewers, the, 68, 155

Minneapolis Millers, the, 119

minor-league baseball, 43, 123

Mize, Johnny, 105

Mockler, Stan, 70

Montreal Star, 67

Moore, Euel, 37–38; as an older player, 44

Moore, Gene, 5, 10, 13, 17, 46, 104; in the first game of the 1944 World Series, 74; in the fourth game of the 1944 World Series, 133–34, 137; in the second game of the 1944 World Series, 93; in the third game of the 1944 World Series, 130

Moore, Terry, 81, 98

movie industry, 113

Muckerman, Richard, 143
Mulcahy, Hugh, 115
Muncrief, Bob, 7, 36, 47; as an older
    player, 44
Munger, George, 80
Murphy, Johnny, 45
Musial, Dickie, 107
Musial, Geraldine, 147
Musial, Lillian, 102–3, 105, 107, 108–9,
    147
Musial, Lukasz, 101–2, 107, 148
Musial, Stan, 57, 58, 61, 80, 121, 146, 157;
    assessment of the St. Louis Browns,
    86–87; career after playing baseball,
    150–51; family and background of,
    100–103; in the first game of the 1944
    World Series, 74–76; first game with
    the St. Louis Cardinals, 104–5; in the
    fourth game of the 1944 World Series,
    133, 139; involvement in politics, 150;
    and Marty Marion, 105, 106; military
    service of, 107, 110, 147–49; modesty
    of, 140; salary of, 83, 98–100, 106–7;
    signs with the St. Louis Cardinals,
    103–4; talent of, 83, 85, 86, 90, 105–6,
    108–9, 149–50; teams interested in,
    103–4
Mutual Radio Network, 66

National League pennant, 6, 13, 17, 46,
    56, 80, 115
National Temperance and Prohibition
    Council, 112
Negro Giants, the, 43
Newhouser, Hal, 2, 51
New Orleans Pelicans, the, 37
newsreels of the 1944 World Series, 67–
    68
Newsweek, 66
New York Daily News, 121–22
New York Giants, the, 18, 38, 44–45,
    103, 108; Mel Ott of, 113, 126; spring
    training location, 119
New York Times coverage: of athletes in
    the military, 118; of baseball, 14, 37,
    42; of the temperance movement, 112;

of the 1944 World Series, 59, 77, 96,
    97, 127, 129, 131, 133, 135, 139–40
New York Yankees, the, 1–2, 5, 23, 25, 46,
    80, 90, 106, 118, 125, 146, 155; fourth
    game against the St. Louis Browns,
    9–15; 4-F players, 45; interest in Stan
    Musial, 103; media coverage of, 46;
    1944 season before the World Series,
    49, 53–54; spring training location,
    120; World Series against other New
    York teams, 18; 1943 World Series
    team, 11
Niggeling, Johnny, 49
night baseball, 116
Nixon, Richard, 144
Nuxhall, Joe, 124

Oakland Oaks, 37
O'Brien, Jerry, 147
O'Dea, Ken, 76, 80, 96, 97
O'Doul, Lefty, 37
O'Hara, John, 73
oil shortages during World War II, 122
Oliver, Porky, 116
O'Neill, Steve, 7
Ostermueller, Fritz, 62–63
Ott, Mel, 113, 126
Owen, Mickey, 57, 129
owners: St. Louis Browns, 14, 20–26, 54,
    58, 143, 150, 155; St. Louis Cardinals,
    80, *81*, 157

Page, Joe, 67
Paige, Satchel, 43
part-time baseball players, 5, 30–31, 33,
    123–24, 144
Patton, George S., 48
Paul, Alexander, 70–71
Pearl Harbor attack, 26, 107, 116, 117
Pennantitis, 53
Perfectos, Louis, 157
Pesky, Johnny, 146
Peters, Arthur, 142
Philadelphia Athletics, the, 4, 9, 123, 136,
    139, 144

Philadelphia Phillies, the, 86, 121, 128, 146
Picone, Mario, 124
Pinder, John, 125
Pipgras, George, 137
Pittsburgh Pirates, the, 103, 106, 119, 126, 149–50
Pollet, Howie, 145
popularity of baseball, 43, 114–15
Potter, Nelson, 7, *29*, 31, 33–34, 36, 41, 46, 87, 91; as an older player, 44; in the fourth game of the 1944 World Series, 137, 139; media coverage of, 62; in the 1944 season opener, 47; in the second game of the 1944 World Series, 91–93, 96; superstitiousness of, 90; suspension of, 50
Povich, Shirley, 49–50
Prohibition, 111–12
Prohibitionist Party, 112

Queen, Mel, 10, 11, 12, 13

rationing during World War II, 120–21
Reiser, Pete, 147
Reynolds, Allie, 48
Rice, Grantland, 67
Richardson, James Eugene, 39
Rickey, Branch, 157; and the Brooklyn Dodgers, 90, 98; concern about the minor leagues, 43, 123; on drafting of baseball players by the military, 113; on night baseball, 116; and the St. Louis Cardinals, 20, *21*, 95; and Stan Musial, 99–100, 105
Riddle, Elmer, 85
Ridley, Walter, 69
Rizzuto, Phil, 125
Robertson, Orlo, 67
Robeson, Paul, 43
Robinson, Aaron, 45
Robinson, Jackie, 20
Robison, Frank, 157
Robison, Stanley, 157
Rolfe, Red, 45
Rommel, Ed, 9

Roosevelt, Franklin, 42, 90, 111, 137; on the importance of baseball, 116–17
Root, Charlie, 137
Rose, Pete, 150
Rowe, Schoolboy, 125
Rowland, Clarence, 123
Royal, Chip, 52
rubber shortages during World War II, 121–22
Ruffing, Red, 45
Russell, James K., 103
Russo, Marius, 45
Ruth, Babe, 18, 116, 121, 137, 155

Saigh, Fred, 151
Sanders, Ray, 60, 74–75, 76, 80; in the fourth game of the 1944 World Series, 133–35, 139; in the third game of the 1944 World Series, 129–30
San Francisco Seals, the, 37
Scanlon, Bobby, 14, 15, 69–70
Schmidt, Freddy, 61, 130
Schneider, Bill, 68
Sears, Ken, 45
Sears, Ziggy, 136
second game of the 1944 World Series, 90–97
Selective Service System (sss), 110–11, 123
Sewell, James Luther "Luke": and the 1944 American League pennant, 3, 7, 9, 10, 13, 16–17, 54–55; analysis of the 1944 World Series, 141; belief in the St. Louis Browns, 53–54, 77; firing of, 143–44; playing career of, 24–25, 73; praise for, 140; recruitment of players by, 30–36, 39–41, 44, 46; and the second game of the 1944 World Series, 97; selected as manager for the St. Louis Browns, 24–26; strategy for the 1944 season, 47–48, 49–50; strategy for the 1944 World Series, 62–65, 127, 128, 133, 139; training program instituted by, 27–30; and U. S. O. shows, 126
Sewell, Joe, 69
Shartak, Mike, 36

Douglas MacArthur and, 41, 47; General George S. Patton and, 48; German war prisoners during, 42, 43–44; major events, 124–25; movie industry during, 113; oil shortages during, 122; optimism during, 42; Pearl Harbor attack during, 26, 107, 116, 117; rationing during, 120–21; religious missionaries during, 70–71; rubber shortages during, 121–22; shortage of baseball players during, 45, 80, 85, 110; spring training locations

during, 118–19; travel restrictions during, 59, 118–21. *See also* military, the

Wright, Mel, 146
Wunderlich, Jerry, 103
Wyatt, Whit, 88–89

Zahn, Charles H., 68
Zarilla, Al, 10, 36, 46, 128–31, 136
Zivic, Fritzie, 116
Zoldak, Sam, 7, 39, 44
Zoller, Jack, 123